Chilkoot Pass

Chilkoot Pass

The Most Famous Trail in the North

Revised and Expanded Edition

Archie Satterfield

Alaska Northwest Publishing Company

Anchorage, Alaska

First Edition 1973
Revised and Expanded Edition 1978
Sixth Printing 1988

Library of Congress cataloging in publication data:
Satterfield, Archie.
    Chilkoot Pass, the most famous trail in the North.
    First ed. published in 1973 under title: Chilkoot
Past, then and now.
    Bibliography: p.
    Includes index.
    1. Chilkoot Trail.   2. Klondike gold fields.
3. Skagway, Alaska—History.   I. Title.
F1095.K5S37   1978   917.19′1   78-9771
ISBN 0-88240-109-2

Design by Jon.Hersh
Cover illustration by Val Paul Taylor

Alaska Northwest Publishing Company
Box 93370, Anchorage, Alaska 99509-3370

Printed in U.S.A.

The Photographs: *The historical photographs are from the University of Washington
Special Collection, the Washington State Historical Society and the Seattle Historical
Society. All other photographs are by the author, or as credited.*

To Joyce, who hiked the Chilkoot, too.

CONTENTS

Preface

PREFACE
to the Revised and Expanded Edition

How simple life would be for writers if history stopped in its tracks the moment a book like this was published. But that isn't the way it works, and the march of history demands revision.

The Klondike Gold Rush National Historical Park was in the planning stage when I first wrote this book, and at the time there was some reason for doubt that the park would ever come into being. But fortunately it was created in 1976, and this latest revised edition takes into account the new facilities and changes brought about by the formation of the park. I hope the park will one day be extended all the way down from Chilkoot Pass to Dawson City in the Yukon Territory, or even beyond back into Alaska to Fortymile and Circle City.

Other major changes have been made in this edition, too. I added a completely new chapter on the big strike itself, and another on Seattle's role in the gold rush because the story of the Klondike—and Chilkoot Pass—is incomplete without it. Seattle was part of the most important corridor to the Klondike and one of the biggest boosters of the Chilkoot route. This fact is clearly reflected in the establishment of a unit of the Klondike Gold Rush National Historical Park in Seattle.

I have also added new photographs, both historical and current, and removed some that were outdated or of lesser importance. A number of corrections have been made, and there are some changes in emphasis for purposes of clarification. One of the most important changes for the hiker is the improved map.

I am indebted to Wendy Wolf for her suggestions for the map and descriptions of the trail today, and also to Manfred and Christine Hedgecock. Others who have helped in this revision are R.W. Sutton of Parks Canada; Clay Anderson of the Klondike Gold Rush National Historical Park in Skagway; James A. "Rocky" Richardson, former regional chief of interpretation, Pacific Northwest Region, National Park Service, and those, too numerous to name, who have contacted me regarding the book since it was first published. The contributions made by these many individuals have been invaluable, but if any inaccuracies remain, the fault is solely mine, not theirs.

Archie Satterfield
Seattle, 1987

PART I:
THE GLORY DAYS

CHAPTER 1
BEGINNINGS

The Taiya River flattens out and grows silent as it passes the Dyea townsite. Athough Dyea is within sight of the saltwater of Lynn Canal, it is too far back on the tidelands for the lapping of waves to reach one's ears. Here and there a few scattered ruins of buildings and three rows of stubs, which once were pilings, stretch down the flats toward the sea. Two cemeteries are back in the woods, well tended but out of sight. Plump, glossy-coated horses graze and romp across the tongue of green land that stretches a little further south each year as the Taiya drops its load of glacial silt in the flat estuary.

This place, dominated by the silence of history, is where the Chilkoot Trail begins.

At no other time or place in recorded history did so many people voluntarily subject themselves to so much agony and misery and death—and glory—than those twenty to thirty thousand who crossed the Chilkoot Pass on their way to the Klondike goldfields in 1897-98. It can only be compared with an army in retreat or refugees in flight, victims of the madness attending war. Chilkoot was the madness attending gold.

The Chilkoot Trail has been called the "meanest 32 miles in history" by students of the gold rush, and today some are calling that same trail the "most beautiful 32 miles in Alaska and British Columbia" and the "world's longest museum." Obviously, it is still a very personal experience.

Nobody knows how long the trail was used by Indians before the first white men arrived at the Yukon headwaters after sailing to the very northern tip of the Inside Passage from Puget Sound. But when the whites did arrive, the Chilkats, a branch of the Tlingit nation, were enjoying a virtual monopoly on trade with the Nahane, or Stick Indians living along the Yukon River and the vast, beautiful lakes that form its headwaters. The Sticks trapped and exchanged pelts for fish oil and other sea products from the Chilkats, and Chilkoot Pass, that narrow slash in the foggy and windy Coast Range was the only practical route for the traders. Generally speaking, the Chilkats were aggressive and domineering and the Sticks mild and docile. This comparison was made by several early visitors to the area and during the stampede to the Klondike, after the Sticks began working as packers, the prospectors often noted that if a Chilkat fell or injured himself, other members of his band offered no sympathy. Conversely, the Sticks were considerate and helpful among themselves.

Although only some 27 miles of land separates Lynn Canal and the navigable waters of the Yukon at Lake Lindeman, it was nearly 50 years after the arrival of the first white man in the Yukon drainage before Chilkoot Pass became the common route.

Hotcakes were constant items on menus.

3

First into the region were the British and Canadians for the Hudson's Bay Co., exploring, trapping and establishing a series of posts and forts along the river and its major tributaries. They came from the Pacific Ocean up the Yukon and west from the interior of Canada, and bought furs from the Chilkats at tidewater. The whites were a new element in the long-established trade patterns of the Tlingits, who felt that routes in their territory should be protected because whoever ruled them also ruled the trade. To underline their claim, in 1852 a band went up the Chilkat Valley, later the Dalton Trail, to Fort Selkirk at the mouth of the Pelly, and burned it to the ground.

But the tide already had turned against them. Former Hudson's Bay employees and missionaries had found evidence of gold fields around the Yukon River, and gold rushes were as much a part of Western civilization as Christianity. Soon prospectors began arriving, one or two at a time, slowly working their way farther and farther back into the wilderness toward the Arctic Circle.

Possibly the first white to cross Chilkoot Pass, in either 1874 or 1875, was one of those men who make a vocation of solitude. His name was George Holt and that is almost all we know about him. He said he found gold but apparently brought none out. The Indians killed him in 1886, at the Alaska Commercial Company's trading post on Knik Arm, near present-day Anchorage.

In 1879 three prospectors tried to go over the pass and were turned back by the Indians. The next year a party of 19 miners appealed to Commander Beardslee of the U.S.S. *Jamestown* at Sitka for assistance in opening the route to them. The miners, headed by an old California prospector named Edmund Bean, was experienced and Beardslee agreed. When they left Sitka on May 20, in several small boats, the commander sent along a steam launch with Lieut. E. P. McClellan in charge.

The launch carried two other Navy officers, a pilot, a doctor, 13 sailors and two Indian interpreters. The interpreters must have done their work well because the Chilkats not only agreed to let the miners through, but to pack for them. The Navy boat did, however, carry a Gatling gun, and rifles and small arms for the entire crew, which may have helped in the negotiations.

The miners left tidewater on May 29. On June 17 Bean wrote to Beardslee and hired an Indian postman to carry out the letter. It said they were camped on the shore of a lake, building boats.

4

After dinner there was always time to wonder what they had gotten themselves into.

During the summer they found some gold but nothing big. On November 15, Commander Henry Glass, who had succeeded Beardslee at Sitka, noted that "all the miners are back from the Yukon."

Two other prospectors, John McKenzie and "Slim Jim" Winn, tried to go to the interior on their own, using liquor as their entrance fee. It only got them in trouble and they were chased out.

In 1880 gold was discovered at Juneau, and in 1881 on Big Salmon. In 1882 prospectors began heading up Lynn Canal again and over Chilkoot Pass. The trickle increased to a steady stream and the deluge wasn't too far away. Fortymile was founded in 1886, and Circle City in 1894-95.

The years 1897-98 are so emphasized in history as the gold-rush years, that the period before is slighted. There was no accurate count taken, of course, but each summer more and more prospectors entered the Yukon either by way of St. Michael and up the Yukon by the all-water route, or over Chilkoot Pass and down the river. There is evidence that more than a thousand used Chilkoot Pass before the great stampede.

Many prospected the upper reaches of the river, working the streams during summer months, then packing back up the river and chain of lakes, over the pass and down to tidewater to winter along the forested islands of Southeast Alaska. Some holed up in the interior, but there were no significant strikes to encourage town building. Finally paydirt was struck on the Klondike River watershed in 1896.

Although there always will be other versions, other rumors and other claims of discovery on the Klondike, the official version is that Robert Henderson gets the credit.

The Henderson version is that he found a stream rich with gold and told another white man, George Washington Carmack, who was at Five Finger Rapids with his Indian wife and her band of Stick Indians. But in telling Carmack, Henderson said he wanted no Indians staking claims. He also refused to share his tobacco with them.

A short time later Carmack and his brothers-in-law, Skookum Jim and Tagish Charley, made the big strike, one of the biggest in history. They broke the miners' code by not telling Henderson. By the time he heard, all the claims worth staking were taken. His superior attitude toward the Indians had cost him a fortune.

CHAPTER 2
SCHWATKA'S JOURNEY

Interest in the Yukon River drainage had grown steadily between 1880 and 1895. Civil government for Alaska was established in 1884, giving the Treasury Department and the navy official roles. But since the army had established a reputation for exploration with Lewis and Clark, it was the army that sent one of the first major explorations over Chilkoot Pass and into Canada. Typically, in that era of Manifest Destiny and border disputes with America's neighbors, the first military expedition was made without prior consent or even notification to Canada.

The plan was forwarded with persistence by Brig. Gen. Nelson A. Miles, Commander of the Department of Columbia at Vancouver Barracks in Washington Territory. Miles, like many military leaders and bureaucrats, wanted to expand his realm of influence, preferably north. He had been told that Alaska was not his responsibility, but he believed it should be, and that the army should lead exploration into the far northwestern slice of the continent.

In 1881 he had asked for and was denied an appropriation of $68,000 to explore Alaska. The following year, he visited Southeast Alaska anyway. It only whetted his appetite to have the North explored, and on his return he organized a small, clandestine expedition.

His Lewis-and-Clark was a young aide, Lieut. Frederick Schwatka. A native of Illinois, Schwatka had worked as a printer and attended Willamette University in Oregon before graduating from the U.S. Military Academy in 1871. He later studied law and medicine, was admitted to the Nebraska bar and received a medical degree from New York's Bellevue Hospital Medical College. To round out his qualifications, he had led a search in the Canadian Arctic in 1879-80 for the long-lost Sir John Franklin expedition.

Schwatka's party of six men, in the lieutenant's words, "stole away like a thief in the night, with less money than was afterward spent to publish its report." On May 22, 1883, they boarded the fleet collier *Victoria* at Portland, with a comprehensive set of orders from Gen. Miles reminiscent of those issued to Lewis and Clark by Thomas Jefferson.

The party was to ascertain the number, character and disposi-

Sled dogs were pressed into service with travois during the summer months of the stampede.

tion of the Indians; their relations with each other; their feeling toward the Russian government; their attitude toward the United States. Schwatka was to study the Indians' way of life and their method of communicating between regions. He was to report on the types of weapons used by the Indians and where and how they secured them.

The party, which consisted of a surgeon, a mapmaker, three enlisted men and a civilian, also was ordered to study the terrain and the best means of "employing and sustaining a military force in the territory, if the occasion should arise," with special inquiry as to the kind and extent of the "native grasses" for horses, mules and cattle.

Schwatka's journal and reports tell one of the first accounts on record of a Chilkoot Pass crossing. His briefing by Carl Spuhn,

LAROCHE

9

superintendent of the Northwest Trading Co.'s salmon cannery at Pyramid Harbor, tipped him off to the reputation of the Chilkat Indians' prowess as packers. Spuhn told Schwatka the Indians were accustomed to carrying 100 pounds, and one packer had carried 160 pounds over the pass. The established fee for packing over the pass was $9 to $12 per 100 pounds, with no discounts for volume.

When the exploring party arrived at the head of Lynn Canal, they had to lighter their goods ashore from the Northwest Trading Co.'s launch, *Louise*. Schwatka set up camp about a mile from the head of the inlet. Chilkats were camped nearby, perhaps to meet the Sticks for trading purposes.

Schwatka's description of the area shows how little it has changed in spite of all the events that followed. He described it as being in a valley that was about a half-mile to three-quarters of a mile across, bounded by steep mountains rising 5,000 feet or more. The river was strewn with boulders, sand and gravel, "with here and there groves of poplars, willows of several varieties, and birch." The Taiya River was swift and from 30 to 75 yards wide to the head of canoe navigation at a cascade 8 miles from its mouth (later to be Canyon City's site). It frequently divided into channels, and in many places it could be forded.

The hike was planned as carefully as a military campaign. Most of the gear was carried in canoes from Camp No. 1 to the cascade 6 miles upriver. When the river had to be forded, Schwatka and his party rode across on packers' backs, which he airily explained away by saying the Indians' legs were "more used to the ice water just from the glacier beds on the hilltops."

The party had no particular problems reaching the Canyon City site. Beyond there, Schwatka complained of "great windrows and avalanches of broken bowlders and shattered stones varying in size from a person's head to the size of a small house." Willows and birches were misshapen and bent as they grew out of the "bowlder barricades," indicating recent avalanches in the area between Sheep Camp and Stone House.

It took them 12 hours to cover the 6 miles between Canyon City and Stone House, where they camped their second night on the trail. Schwatka said the natives crawled under the massive chunks of granite to sleep out of the snow.

There was nothing particularly remarkable about Schwatka's

ascent over the pass, except that he named it Perrier Pass in honor of Col. J. Perrier of the French Geographical Society. Fortunately, the name did not stick and it has remained the Chilkoot.

Schwatka, however, did establish the names of several other places along the trail to the Klondike. He named Lake Lindeman for Dr. Lindemann, secretary to the Bremen Geographical Society. Usage corrupted the name to its present single "n" on the end, although during the gold rush, it was frequently called "Linderman," perhaps because a Bostonian pronounced it and another stampeder passed it on.

Schwatka also named Lake Bennett for James Gordon Bennett of the *New York Herald*, and Miles Canyon* for his superior officer and sponsor of the expedition. The remainder of his trip down to St. Michael was relatively uneventful, and the stretch of the Yukon between Nukluklayet and St. Michael was made aboard the Alaska Commercial Co. steamer *Yukon*.

The Canadian government was understandably irritated to hear of his expedition after it was completed—most likely through books Schwatka later wrote. But many of the names he affixed to geographical features survived. Apparently all was forgiven by the Canadians, because they named the man-made lake at White-horse in honor of Schwatka.

*Some sources report Schwatka first named Miles Canyon, "Grand Canyon."

CHAPTER 3
DISCOVERIES

Four years later a more authorized expedition was made into the area. William Ogilvie was ordered by the Canadian government to survey the 141st meridian to establish the national boundary where it crossed the Yukon River. He also was to run the line north from Chilkat Inlet to determine the boundary along the Coast Range.

The border question was the result of the 1825 Convention between Great Britain and Russia setting boundaries, which were neither surveyed nor questioned until after Russia ceded Alaska to the United States in the U.S.-Russia Convention of 1867. But with the increased activity in trapping and mining in northwestern Canada and the still unorganized territory of Alaska, the need for definite boundaries became apparent.

The 141st meridian wasn't challenged, but the boundary down the Coast Range was. The Convention of 1825, impossible to render into common, conversational English, read:

> whereas, where the summit of the mountains which shall extend in a direction parallel to the coast, from the fifty-sixth degree of north latitude to the point of intersection on the 141st degree west longitude shall prove to be of the distance of more than ten marine leagues from the ocean the limit between British possessions and the line of the coast, which is to belong to Russia . . . shall form a line parallel to the sinuosities of the coast, and which shall never exceed the distance of ten marine leagues therefrom. . . .

Simply put, the Canadians believed their boundaries extended to the head of Lynn Canal and the Taiya estuary. The Americans disagreed, maintaining that Canada had no access to the sea. The Americans also believed their boundary extended beyond the pass and down as far as Lake Bennett. A stream of prospectors, traders, trappers and an occasional scoundrel were heading into the Yukon drainage at an increasing rate. Where customs posts were set up and duties collected by both nations, would establish the international boundary.

Between Schwatka's trip in 1883 and Ogilvie's arrival at the Taiya estuary in the summer of 1887, a trading post was established at Dyea by one of the West's more colorful characters, John J. Healy, and a partner, Edgar Wilson. George Dickenson, who had lived among the Chilkats, was hired as translator and storekeeper.

Healy had a long, colorful career along the Montana-Canadian border. He had established a whiskey fort named Fort Whoop-up, and at one time had put down a takeover attempt by a gang of wolf hunters by holding a lighted cigar near enough to a keg of gunpowder to convince them he would kill himself and them before yielding.

He later became known for another hard-nosed stance at Fortymile. He refused to accept the ruling of a miners' court that he pay a hired girl a year's wages because he had locked her out of the house for staying out all night. Rather than yield, Healy asked for protection from an old friend from the Whoop-up country, Samuel B. Steele, a superintendent in the Royal North-West Mounted Police. Steele complied, which led Healy to be accused by some of helping to bring the unwanted restrictions of civilization into the Yukon.

Ogilvie had hired 120 Chilkat packers at $10 a hundred pounds to pack his gear over Chilkoot Pass to Lake Lindeman. He used two Peterborough canoes to shuttle the equipment down to Lake Bennett.

Ogilvie's trip over Chilkoot Pass was an important one. Not only did he measure the height of the pass (3,502 by his figures, but later established as 3,739 feet) and Lake Lindeman (2,141 feet), he also introduced into the pages of history a cluster of important names—Capt. William Moore, Carmack and his wife Kate, and her brother Skookum Jim.

Moore was 65 and had lived a full life after leaving his native Germany for the sea. He migrated to the United States and operated towboats on the Lower Mississippi, fought in the Mexican War and prospected in California, on the Fraser, the Cariboo and the Cassiar. But now he was getting old, his home had been sold to pay creditors in Victoria and he was looking for one more chance to strike it rich.

Moore, like Ogilvie, had heard of another pass into the Yukon headwaters. Both wanted to find it, Moore for a chance to build a town to serve the gold rush he believed was going to occur, and Ogilvie because he was a man of infinite curiosity and wanted to add it to his list of discoveries.

He sent Moore up the Skagway River to find it. With Moore

When John Muir was asked to describe the situation at Skagway and Dyea for a magazine, he declined, saying the gold rush looked like a hill of ants someone had stirred up with a stick. The frantic scenes on the twin waterfronts probably matched his description.

was Skookum Jim, an extremely strong Stick Indian (*skookum* was jargon for strong). Ogilvie also had hired a white man who lived just downstream from the Yukon's confluence with the Little Salmon River with his wife Kate, Skookum Jim's sister. This white man, Carmack, had a pump organ in his home and a library that included scientific and philosophic books. It was Carmack who induced the Sticks to overcome their fear of the coastal tribes and pack Ogilvie's gear from Crater Lake to Lake Lindeman at $5 a hundred pounds.

Moore and Skookum Jim took off alone and went up the Skagway River through the pass. They joined Ogilvie at Lake Lindeman. The new pass was named for Thomas White, Ogilvie's superior.

The trek convinced Moore, an experienced road builder, that a rail line could be built through White Pass because it lacked the steep summit climb of Chilkoot. The fact that it was some 7 or 8 miles longer was of no consequence.

ASAHEL CURTIS

15

Moore left Ogilvie's party and returned with his son to tidewater. They staked a homestead claim at the mouth of the Skagway River and prepared for the gold rush by building a dock out into deep water.

During this period there had been strikes of varying importance along the Yukon. A minor one had been made on the Stewart River. In 1886 the first coarse gold was discovered on the Fortymile River, indicating that a lode was close by. (Rivers were named for their distance from old Fort Reliance, which was only a few miles downriver from the confluence of the Yukon and Klondike.)

Until then nobody had a good reason for crossing Chilkoot Pass in the dead of winter. However, Arthur Harper, in charge of a trading post at the mouth of the Stewart River, realized the importance of the find at Fortymile. He knew it would bring more miners to the country and more supplies would be needed. His associate, Leroy Napoleon McQuesten, was already on his way to San Francisco, though, to put in a normal order for the coming year.

Harper therefore hired Tom Williams to carry a letter to the head of Lynn Canal and find some way of forwarding it to McQuesten to let him know about the Fortymile strike. Williams took other mail from the trading post and Fort Nelson, and accompanied by an Indian boy named Bob, who helped with the dogs and camp work, headed for the pass.

They fought their way over the ice-choked river, spending more time wrestling the sled than if they had walked. By the time they reached Chilkoot Pass they had killed all their dogs for food and were reduced to eating dry flour. Between Crater Lake and the summit a storm forced them to stay several days in a snow cave, their toes and fingers turning white with frostbite.

When the storm cleared, Williams was unable to walk unassisted. The boy helped him down to Sheep Camp, where they found a party of hunters who fed them, put Williams on a sled and took the pair to Dyea. The miners questioned Williams about his seemingly foolhardy attempt to cross the pass in winter but he would say only that he was on a secret mission. He pleaded with them to go out and find the mail, which had been abandoned. Then he died.

The Indian boy did not speak much English but the miners

learned from him that the mission concerned a gold discovery. The boy picked bits of coal out of the scuttle to show how big the nuggets were.

The big stampede still didn't materialize, but the Fortymile strike increased the volume of foot traffic coming through Dyea. By the following summer at least 1,000 prospectors were working the gravel bars and tributaries of the Yukon.

Clearly the stage was still being set for a much larger production. But only a few were aware of it. It was the traders who saw the grand scheme; the prospectors were too busy with their own dreams of wealth and past failures to think far beyond the next stream or the next unnamed tributary. Some were becoming moderately wealthy, but the big strike, the El Dorado, still eluded them.

The traders were patient men. They would stay with the prospectors and continue grubstaking them each spring and settling their disputes during the long, tedious winters.

It wasn't until 1896 on Rabbit Creek, an insignificant tributary of the Klondike River, that the traders' patience was rewarded. That was the tragedy of Robert Henderson and the glory of Ogilvie's former employees, Carmack and his brothers-in-law, Skookum Jim and Tagish Charley.

When the 68 prospectors who boarded the S.S. *Portland* laden with gold reached Seattle on July 17, 1897, the stampede began. It surpassed even the wildest dreams of traders Al Mayo, McQuesten, Healy and Joe Ladue, who founded Dawson City. The gold rush became a form of madness, a continental insanity, a lemminglike migration to the last unfilled frontier on the continent. The Klondike gold rush, the greatest in history, had begun.

CHAPTER 4
CHILKOOT THEN

Chilkoot Pass is the dominant symbol of the Klondike gold rush of 1897-98. Much more than the gaudy honky-tonk image we have of Dawson City and the miserable goldfields a few miles outside town, Chilkoot Pass some 600 miles from the Klondike lodges itself in the mind, making the remainder of the trek and the fortunes earned and lost anticlimactic.

The most popular and most sensible route to the Klondike was up the Inside Passage from Puget Sound to Skagway and its sister city of Dyea, at the extreme tip of the slender Lynn Canal. From Skagway some took the White Pass route 40 miles to Lake Bennett, but most went by way of Dyea over Chilkoot Pass the 26 miles to Lake Lindeman. Of the 1,600-odd miles from Puget Sound to Dawson City, only these miles were on foot.

In spite of hundreds of items lining the Chilkoot Trail today as evidence of that last great stampede for gold, the hiker over the pass finds it difficult to believe the gold rush ever occurred. Once believed, it is equally difficult to define the chemistry that caused at least 100,000 men—and women—to start out on the gold rush, and the festive mood of renewed self-confidence it created all across North America and much of the Western Hemisphere.

There are hints and clues but no absolutes. The national treasury had been virtually drained of gold. The gold standard had played a major role in the 1896 presidential campaign between McKinley and Bryan. The nation was in the depths of a depression that had no apparent end. The rich were extremely rich and the poor extremely poor. There were no public funds set aside for such amenities as social security, workers compensation, unemployment insurance, food stamps and other guarantees against financial ruin and starvation.

A national restlessness was set into motion by the gold rush, and it gave vent to the feeling that the country should get moving again. It offered hundreds of thousands of square miles of open country, a new frontier to cross and conquer. It became the last great migratory impulse for North America. It was a safety valve, the releasing of the biological need to migrate.

To some, it was simply something to do to relieve the feeling of boredom the past 3 or 4 years had imposed on people. Otherwise, everyone who had gone on the stampede would have begun digging for gold as soon as they arrived in Dawson City. But contemporary accounts show that the majority of stampeders did not even go out to the goldfields; instead, they milled around Dawson City for awhile, then went home.

When those stampeders, or "argonauts" as some called themselves, returned home, it was Chilkoot Pass they remembered. Undoubtedly it has become the most famous pass in North America, and perhaps the entire Western Hemisphere. As hikers today will testify, it has a reputation for savagery it does not deserve—that is, when it is hiked in the summer months.

Skagway began to blossom that fall with planks strung along the street for sidewalks.

ASAHEL CURTIS

19

A major difference is that today hikers go over the trail carrying lightweight packs, dehydrated food and wearing modern lug-soled boots. They hike the trail to Lake Bennett and then board the train. It wasn't nearly that simple in the gold rush.

In the first place, the Royal North-West Mounted Police required a year's supply of food for each person entering Canada. The stampeders had to carry roughly a ton of gear from tidewater to the Yukon headwaters at Lake Lindeman or Lake Bennett. They could carry it themselves, or if they had enough money, hire packers. Later in the stampede they could have it hauled by

The steamer Willamette, *formerly a collier, was outfitted and claimed to have room for 1,000 stampeders aboard. It was a dubious claim.*

wagon the first 7 miles to Canyon City, then by aerial tramway over the pass to Crater Lake. From there they could have it ferried the length of Crater Lake by cargo canoe, by wagon to Long Lake, then by canoe or boat to Deep Lake and overland again to Lake Lindeman. Obviously, those who paid others to bear their burden paid dearly for the luxury.

If they carried everything themselves, shuttling their loads from cache to cache, they had to hike as much as 1,000 miles before they were ready to build boats and float to Dawson City.

To describe the trail before the stampede, one must rely on accounts by men such as Schwatka and Ogilvie, neither of whom went into great detail because they had nothing to be impressed

ASAHEL CURTIS

about. To them, it was just another tramp through the wilderness. Our attitude most likely would be the same were it not for the human folly and heroism displayed during that one year.

The original route was up the stream bed, sometimes into the edge of the forest where the ground was flat and the underbrush thin. The stream had to be forded numerous times, but in many places it was shallow. Other than cold, wet feet, it presented little difficulty. Wagons and canoes could be used.

About 7 miles from Dyea the canyon narrowed and rapids formed, ending the use of wagons and boats. From here on, stampeders had to fight their way through the dense coastal timber, over moss-slickened moraine, giant devil's club and occasionally they had to wade back out into the stream bed when the granite cliffs dropped straight down to the river's edge. The trail ascended the cliff through a steep notch, only to drop back down to the rocky valley floor again.

After 5 miles of this, they reached the first wide, level spot in the canyon. Here, according to uncertain records, sheep (or, more likely here, mountain goat) hunters came to camp. Another version is that an early-arrival for the gold rush drove a band of sheep over the pass and camped there. At any rate, it has always been called Sheep Camp. It is the last stop in the forest before emerging into the open, windy and usually rainy area of the pass itself.

Just beyond Sheep Camp the trail becomes steep, and gains 1,000 feet in elevation in the next 2 miles. Timber line is at the 1,900-foot level, and snow covers the rocks until July. This area is known as Long Hill and terminates at Stone House, already mentioned.

The trail still follows the Taiya, by now no more than a swift brook fed by snowfields. The trail goes up and down slightly, gaining still more elevation until it drops down into a little bowl of boulders called The Scales. It is surrounded by steep, scree-covered mountains on three sides. Directly ahead—or to be more precise, almost straight up—is Chilkoot Pass itself.

There are three routes over it. To the left is a steep climb over ledges, boulders and short ridges. To the right is a long, winding ravine which is the longest of the three. Dead ahead is a 40-degree scree slope which goes straight up the mountainside to the crest. This was it, the Golden Stairs of Chilkoot Pass.

The photographers soon arrived, and prospectors sent photos home showing them hard at work panning for gold, even if the scenes had to be staged.

The scramble up it was the lesser of three evils, and was the most frequently used route. The left-hand route was almost never used because it was too dangerous, and the other side was used primarily by dog teams and livestock, and named the Petterson Trail after, one would guess, a man named Petterson. The reason for the honor has been lost to us.

Strangely enough, most stampeders found that the summit climb was best made in the dead of winter, partly because steps could be hacked out of the snow. During the summer months, every rock in the scree appeared loose and ready to start a slide. Parties crossing the summit had to be extremely careful, spacing out several yards to minimize the danger of dislodging rocks and thumping those below with boulders. In the winter they could climb it almost nose to heel.

The summit itself is a narrow slash where more often than not clouds are whipped through by the hard winds. For modern-day hikers these foul-weather periods make conversation and comfort impossible. After a quick breather, hikers strike out for Crater Lake just below the crest of the summit.

Crater Lake, as its name implies, is a vast, old volcanic cone about 2 miles long that is filled with unbelievably blue, frigid water. The lake is virtually sterile, supports no aquatic life, and constitutes a portion of the headwaters of the Yukon River. (The Yukon has the distinction of beginning 17 miles from the Pacific

Ocean, but it runs more than 2,000 miles before it finally hits that ocean.)

Shaped like a bent mallet, Crater Lake is free of ice and snow only about 3 months of the year. Much of its shore is loose rocks and boulders which change their location frequently through freezing and thawing action and rockslides of varying intensity from the mountains above. Near the lower end of the lake is a broad, marshy area across which numerous streams flow, but most of the trail past the lake goes across the boulders. The stampeders, who used this spot as a camp site, cut and placed poles on the ground in the marsh to serve as bases for their tents.

Another small lake is just below the tip of Crater Lake. It is too small to rate a formal name, although some call it Blue Lake and others, Morrow Lake. The landscape opens slightly along this area, but closes up again as the stream between the lakes gains volume and momentum. The stream cuts through a sheer canyon, and the trail is again reduced to a scramble over loose talus and scree for a quarter of a mile.

The canyon ends at the head of Long Lake, a 3-mile-long narrow lake. The trail leaves the water and zigzags back and forth up the mountainside until it reaches a relatively flat shelf beneath the mountaintop. After 3 miles during which the trail passes a series of tarns and tiny ponds, stunted and contorted trees and low-growing berry vines, it drops down a series of switchbacks and emerges at a short stream between Long Lake and Deep Lake. The trail crosses the stream to the west side of the lake, and here is the first wood for fires since leaving Sheep Camp some 11 miles back.

Deep Lake is small and dotted by picturesque islands with trees and underbrush growing from them. Deep Lake empties into a still larger stream, Moose Creek, which abruptly drops down over a series of falls and rapids. The noise made by the rushing water can be heard for miles in either direction. Navigation down the stream is impossible.

The trail swings slightly west from Deep Lake and uphill to a series of ledges and shelves beneath the crest of the canyon. Since the timber on the Canadian side of the pass is thin and uneven, several routes could be taken the remaining 2 miles to Lake Lindeman, where the Chilkoot Trail ends.

Lake Lindeman was surrounded by a fine stand of timber,

enough for several thousand men to build boats and cabins, and chop firewood. Some, after hiking on down to the lake's outlet, decided it would be best to continue another mile to Lake Bennett. A short, deep stream connects the two large lakes, but the stream is a series of rapids. Many who built their boats or rafts at Lindeman safely navigated the rapids but others did not. Consequently, the largest number of tents were pitched on the shores of Lake Bennett.

But beyond this point, nobody had to carry his gear again. From here on, the entire trip to Dawson City was by water.

CHAPTER 5
THE BIG STRIKE

The 1890s may have been a time of gaiety in some parts of the world, but not for many in the United States. The crash of 1893 precipitated the worst economic depression the country had experienced to that time, and the panic bore all the earmarks of a permanent disaster.

Like most of the depressions that century, it was caused by an overexpansion of the railroads, wild speculation by enthusiastic businessmen, and an uneasiness on the part of European business-men that caused them to sell American bonds, which in turn drained gold from the U.S. treasury. By 1894 thousands of businesses had failed and four million men were looking for work. The panic was directly responsible for the success of the Populist Party, which almost pushed William Jennings Bryan into the White House in 1896 and again in 1900.

It was a desperate time, and American citizens had even fewer federal and state social welfare programs to fall back onto than during the Great Depression of the 1930s. One of the most desperate reactions was Gen. Jacob S. Coxey's Industrial Army, formed in 1894 to march on Washington, D.C., and demand that Congress give relief to starving workers. Soon "Coxey's Army" was marching eastward across the nation, stealing railroad equipment, even whole trains, on its way.

One contingent was formed in the Seattle-Tacoma area and a regular army detachment was sent to head them off at Spokane. The group of sixty-odd Coxeyites was unable to get a whole train to themselves, so at the town of Cle Elum they commandeered a coal car and coasted the downgrade toward Ellenburg. They were given the right-of-way, but the tracks leveled off at the Columbia River and one presumes they came to a halt and were caught there.

Another group stole a train near Spokane, and the railroad simply tore up a section of track ahead of them, causing a wreck.

But for the most part, there was little excitement in the Northwest during those lean years. The vast majority of people were more concerned with getting the next meal than solving the problems of the nation. Fortunately, there was enough wild food available on Puget Sound and in the lakes and rivers and forests behind the towns to keep most people from starving. Seattle was still so small—fewer than 50,000 people—that bear and deer could still be killed between Elliott Bay and Lake Washington, and there were enough clams and bottom fish in the Sound, plus migrating salmon in the Duwamish River, for all.

Among the factors that set the stage for the overwhelming response to the Klondike gold rush was the general mood, the mental state, of the whole nation at that particular time. The American Dream had turned into a nightmare for many immigrants. The promise of free land in the West had become a prison with the horizon its walls. People who had first fled Europe, then the filth and corruption of the East Coast cities, found only hard work with no prospect of the milk and honey they had thought the new land offered. The refugees from the industrial society of New York, Boston, Pittsburgh and Cleveland found that clean air and water alone are not enough. The railroads had effectively put an end to the westering mystique; once the west became accessible to all, its attraction and mystery were gone.

Evidence indicates there was a general paranoia sweeping the nation. There were probably as many senseless killings then as now. Insanity and mental breakdown was rampant. Thousands were afflicted with what came to be known as cabin fever, but instead of being trapped in a small cabin by winter, they were trapped by geography and poverty. Some social historians have called the 1890s a period of psychic crisis for the country, and those who survived the Great Depression of the 1930s will understand something of the mood of the 1890s, even though there seemed to be more hope in the 1930s that things would eventually brighten.

There is another similarity between the two periods: Both were ended dramatically, almost overnight, by a single event. Just as the outbreak of World War II ended the Great Depression, the Klondike gold rush ended the depression of the 1890s. The Klondike gold rush began on Saturday, July 17, 1897, and before a week passed, newspapers were announcing the depression was over and money was circulating again.

Gold rushes were as much a part of American life as the problem of leisure time is today. There had been gold rushes to Colorado, Wyoming, Arizona, then the big one of 1849 to California, followed by smaller stampedes to Oregon, Idaho, Washington and British Columbia. There had been a small one or two into Southeastern Alaska, but the big one continued to elude prospectors in the north.

For two decades or more a trickle of prospectors had worked the streams that feed the Yukon River. Some worked up from the estuary on the northwestern coast of Alaska. Others intercepted the river by heading over the Chilkoot Pass route. They found enough gold to keep them coming back season after season, or to build rough cabins at Circle or Fortymile and winter over.

There was also enough gold found in the early years of the 1880s to bring traders in with small steamboats to make a single trip up the river from the coast at St. Michael each summer. A few traders lived among the prospectors and obtained most of their provisions through Seattle merchants, who often owned the paddlewheelers and coastal vessels that called on other Alaskan ports en route to St. Michael.

By the late 1890s, there were perhaps a thousand prospectors, wives, traders and hangers-on along the Yukon River, most of whom were living around Circle, or around Fortymile where the best strike yet had been made. The majority of these prospectors were from the Seattle area, or at least it had been their last address before heading for Alaska. There was also a sampling of Californians and Canadians, a missionary or two and a small detachment of Mounties sent up by the Canadian government to keep the peace, even though nobody was sure then whether Fortymile was in Alaska or Canada. Civilization was creeping into the wilderness almost as though in preparation for the gold rush that fate had in store.

Old-timers from the period delighted in telling how they lived before the gold rush, of how they used a team of tame moose to pull a plow, and when the moose proved unsatifactory, they hired local Indians to pull it. They had their own system of justice, which appeared to work reasonably well, and when it came to food, shelter and firewood, they were scrupulously honest. Cabins had no locks, and gold nuggets left lying around the claim sites or pokes left inside the cabins were as safe as if they were locked in a Wells Fargo vault. Thieves had no place to go.

When the big strike was finally made in August 1896, the towns of Circle and Fortymile and the little creeks where prospectors worked were vacated. Everyone streamed into what became Dawson City to file claims on the streams that fed the Klondike River a few miles up from its confluence with the Yukon. All that autumn and winter they worked, sinking shafts through the permafrost down to bedrock where the gold was. They built cabins, and chopped firewood to heat them and to thaw out shafts in the permafrost to get at the gold. They worked all that winter until the spring thaw carried away the river ice and the two or three paddlewheelers could make their annual 2,000-mile run upriver from St. Michael. Only then would the outside world hear of the strike.

Unfortunately, it has never been recorded what the skippers of the paddlewheelers thought that June of 1897. But when they arrived, the miners were waiting with their sacks, cans and boxes of gold, still wearing their patched and torn clothing, some suffering from scurvy. What a magnificent shock it must have been to those captains.

At St. Michael the now-wealthy miners transferred to two coastal steamers, the *Excelsior*, bound for San Francisco, and the *Portland*, for Seattle. Aboard the *Excelsior* were at least four men and women from Seattle, one of whom was T. S. Lippy, former manager of the Seattle YMCA. He told a reporter in San Francisco that he wound up on that ship, and in the wrong city, because he couldn't get a berth on the *Portland*.

He and his wife brought out at least $50,000, but nevertheless it wasn't a happy trip for them. They had taken a young son with them to the Klondike and he had died during the Yukon winter. Lippy and his wife spoke of the tragedy often; their new wealth had already extracted a heavy price.

The *Excelsior* landed in San Francisco on July 15, 1897, and the

A group of professional packers and their oxen took a rest break beside the Taiya River. The photo was taken early in the stampede, in the summer of 1897.

miners were treated as a curiosity by the city. They were followed by reporters wherever they went. As soon as they struggled down the gangplank with their booty, they surprised hack drivers by demanding that they be taken immediately to the Shelby smelting plant to have their gold assayed and bought. Only then did they go to the Palace Hotel, where they engaged the best suites, had long-overdue baths, bought new clothes and began celebrating.

"The professor [Lippy], since arriving here, has been the recipient of considerable attention, and is surprised at the large number of friends he seems to have in San Francisco," a reporter remarked wryly. "At the Palace Hotel, where the professor and wife are stopping, a continual stream of visitors poured in on them, till they were compelled to call a halt, and instructed the hotel clerk that they would see no more visitors, but to successfully do so, they leave the city tonight for Portland and will arrive in Seattle in a few days."

The story quoted Lippy as saying Seattle must act to get major benefits from the gold rush he was sure would come. The story ran in the first editions of the *Seattle Post-Intelligencer* with a page-one box telling readers to stand by for an extra edition under preparation with the latest news from the Klondike.

Perhaps San Franciscans were too blasé or they thought the miners were exaggerating the extent of the strike way up north near the Arctic Circle. Whatever the cause, the rush didn't materialize. Not yet. But soon it would. When the *Post-Intelligencer* received a dispatch from San Francisco telling about the *Excelsior*'s cargo, the newspaper beat the competition by chartering a tug, the *Sea Lion*, and put one of its best reporters aboard to intercept the *Portland* as it cleared customs at Port Angeles. The reporter's name was Beriah Brown, and it seems unjust that Brown, whose work may be considered to have started that last great gold rush, received not even a byline on his extraordinarily influential piece of journalism. His story constituted the special edition of the *Post-Intelligencer* that July 17, 1897.

ON BOARD STEAMSHIP PORTLAND.
3 A.M. —At 3 o'clock this morning the steamship Portland, from St. Michaels for Seattle, passed up Sound with more than a ton of solid gold on board

and 68 passengers. In the captain's cabin are three chests and a large safe filled with the precious nuggets. The metal is worth nearly $700,000 and the most of it was taken out of the ground in less than three months of last winter. In size the nuggets range from the size of a pea to a guinea egg. Of the 68 miners aboard hardly a man has less than $7,000 and one or two have more than $100,000 in yellow nuggets.

One peculiar feature to be noticed is that the big strikes were made by tenderfeet, while the old and experienced miners of many years' experience are suffering indescribable hardship and privation in Alaska and the Northwest Territory and have only a few thousand dollars to show for their labor. Fortune seemed to smile on the inexperienced men who went into the mining districts late last year, as nearly all of them were the most fortunate. The stories they tell seem too incredulous and far beyond belief. Instances are noted where single individuals have taken out, in two and one-half months, gold to the value of over $150,000.

Clarence Berry, of Fresno, Cal., went to the Yukon in 1894 and prospected several years without success. He returned home last autumn, was married and took his bride to the Klondike last November. He is now on the Portland with $125,000, the result of a winter's work and fortune's smile.

Frank Phiscator, of Baroda, Mich., is another lucky miner. He went to the Klondike last autumn and is now returning with $86,027, having worked two claims with nine men, three months, and he still owns the claims. He was one of the original discoverers of the El Dorado district.

Although most of the passengers are returning home with plenty of gold, they all advise and urge people who contemplate going to the Yukon not to think of taking in less than one ton of grub, and plenty of clothes. While it is a poor man's country, yet the hardships and privations to be encountered by inexperienced persons unused to frontier life is certain to result in much suffering during the winters. They should go prepared with at least a year's supplies.

The rush to the Klondike region commenced late last year and the claims were staked out and worked all winter. Labor was worth $15 a day last winter. Flour sold for $60 a sack and other provisions were proportionately higher. Some of the mine owners attempted to lower the wages to $10 without success. By burning the ground to thaw the gravel, which was hoisted up about twelve feet to the dumps, where it was sluiced and washed in the spring, miners were able to work during the entire winter. In the early part of last month the thermometer ran up to 85 degrees in the shade and in January it was 58 degrees below zero.

The steamer Portland was reported passing Cape Flattery at 3 o'clock yesterday afternoon. The news dispatches from San Francisco announcing the arrival of the Excelsior at that port with many miners and a large quantity of gold has created a public demand for the latest and most authentic news from the gold fields of Alaska.

Realizing the impossibility of the Portland arriving in Seattle before 8 or 9 o'clock this morning, the Post-Intelligencer telegraphed to Manager Libby of the Puget Sound Tugboat Co. at Port Townsend and chartered the tug Sea Lion, Capt. C. W. Sprague to intercept the Portland in the straits so that this paper's representatives could interview the returning miners and lay their stories before the public at the earliest moment.

In The Straits

At 2 o'clock this morning the Portland was stopped in the middle of the straits abreast of Port Angeles by the Sea Lion. As the reporter went over the steamer's side and was met by Capt. Kidston, a crowd of miners gathered about, eager to hear the latest local news. Entering the captain's cabin, the skipper pointed to a corner in which was piled three boxes and a large safe.

$700,000 in Gold

"There, you see those boxes and that safe: well, they contain in round figures over $700,000 in gold, and that metal weighs nearly a ton and a half," was the captain's response to the reporter's question as to the amount of gold that was on board. He continued:

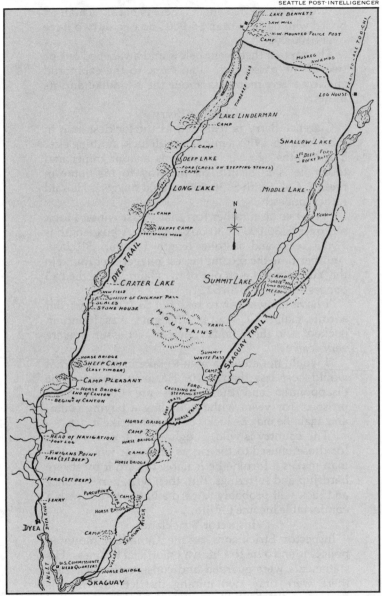

When the gold rush began, newspapers and magazines all over North America began printing special Klondike editions, complete with maps. Some, such as this one, were relatively accurate, with only minor spelling variations.

"Out of the 68 passengers there is hardly a man on board who has less than $5,000 and one or two have over $100,000."

The captain then went below and awakened one or two of the passengers, who came to the cabin and chatted a few moments about the Klondike and its mines.

Clarence Berry

Clarence Berry is regarded as the luckiest man in the Klondike. With a miner it is all luck, nothing else. Ten months ago Mr. Berry was a poor miner and today he is in Seattle on his way to his home in Fresno, Cal., with $130,000 in gold nuggets. He said rather modestly:

"Yes, I've been rather fortunate. Last winter I took out over $130,000 in 30 box lengths. A box length is 12x15 feet, and in one length I found $10,000. Another time the second largest nugget ever found in the Yukon was taken out of my claim; it weighed 13 ounces and was worth $231.

"I have known men to take out $1,000 a day from a drift claim. Of course, the gold was found in pockets, and those finds, you can rest assured, were very scarce.

"I would not advise a man to take in an outfit that would cost less than $500. He must expect to be disappointed and the chances are that he may prospect for years without finding a paying claim, and again he may be lucky enough to strike it rich.

"The country is wild, rough and full of hardships for those unused to the rigors of Arctic winters. If a man makes a fortune he is liable to earn it by severe hardship and sufferings. But, then, grit, perseverance and luck will probably reward a hard worker with a comfortable income for life."

Inspector Strickland

Inspector Strickland, of the Canadian mounted police, is en route to Ottawa on official business. His statements were guarded and conservative. He said there were only two mining districts in what is known as the Klondike section and they are called the Hunker and Bonanza districts. He added:

"When I left Dawson City a month ago there were about 600 claims staked out and there were between

2,000 and 3,000 people in there. We can safely say that there was about $1,500,000 in gold mined last winter. The wages in the mines were $15 a day and the new saw mill paid laborers $10 a day.

"The claims now staked out will afford employment for about 5,000 men, I believe. If a man is strong, healthy and wants to work he can find employment at good wages. Several men worked on an interest or what is termed a 'lay' and during the winter realized from $5,000 to $10,000 apiece. The mines are from 35 to 100 miles from the Alaska boundary."

A Seattle Man

William Stanley, of Seattle, is among the passengers. He left his son in charge of his interests in a couple of claims. He went to the Klondike last year and is now returning with nearly $90,000 in gold.

Henry Anderson, a native of Sweden and well known on the Sound, sold a one-half interest in his claim on El Dorado creek and is coming back to Seattle with $45,000 spot cash, the proceeds of the sale. . . .

The story continued on for several more paragraphs, listing more men aboard the *Portland* and what they brought back. To Brown's credit, he did not write hysterically, and the calm manner in which he laid out the incredible story was probably more effective than had he written a yarn to match the screaming headline over the story ("GOLD! GOLD! GOLD! GOLD!" and "STACKS OF YELLOW METAL!"). He was also conservative in reporting the estimated weight of the gold. When it all was weighed and counted up, it came to more than 2 tons.

Beriah Brown did his work well. Before that day ended, there were lines of people at the ticket offices buying space on the *Portland's* return voyage. The gold rush was under way, and some, familiar with the California rush of 1849 which lured men across the continent and around the Horn, believe the Klondike was the greatest of them all.

CHAPTER 6
SEATTLE FEEDS ON THE RUSH

Shipping had not been a very profitable enterprise during the depression years of the 1890s, and the docks, like the shipyards of Puget Sound, were used as much for storage ("boneyards" some called them) as for the transfer of material to and from ships. The gold rush changed that virtually overnight. Ships of all descriptions were pressed into service, whether they were up to the task or not. It is true that there were government inspectors responsible for ship safety, but they were largely ignored in the stampede.

How else would one explain a ship taking off from Seattle's Elliott Bay without a compass, or another piled so high with goods for the North that the skipper couldn't see straight ahead, or the collier *Roanoke* being fitted out with 600 bunks in the dark, black, filthy hold, or the 45-foot launch *Rustler* with 70 passengers aboard and the captain's only relevant experience was that he had been a milk-wagon driver in San Francisco?

There wasn't a great regard for lives, human or animal. The ancient bark *Colorado* left Seattle on October 29 behind the tug *Pioneer* with 350 horses, 150 cattle and 100 dogs aboard, and a scow alongside with food for them. Newspapers were littered with references to cattle dying before the skyline of Seattle disappeared from view, and several of the animals were dead before the flotilla reached Port Townsend. There were cases involving near mutiny, such as when the old brigantine *Blakely* was loaded and passengers discovered that a herd of horses had been assigned to the dining salon.

The fares, notwithstanding the Seattle Chamber of Commerce's published schedule, represented whatever the steamship lines thought the market would bear, and by the spring of 1898, the fares from Seattle were roughly these:

To Ketchikan and Wrangell (presumably for those trying the Stikine River route, a killer) $30 first class, $20 second class; Juneau, $35 and $22; Dyea, Skagway or Sitka, $50 and $35; and to St. Michael, $150 and $125. Cargo was charged either by weight or dimension, ship's option, and was $12.50 per ton to Skagway, $15 to Dyea (only 8 miles farther), $200 to St. Michael.

The waterfront became the most fascinating place in Seattle as people gathered to watch the longshoremen (who had a successful strike and gained a jump in pay from 40 to 50 cents an hour) loading cargo and animals, and the stampeders boarding the overcrowded ships, many drunk from sampling Seattle's flourishing nightlife. It wasn't unusual for one ship to ram another because so many of the crews and officers were inexperienced, and at times the harbor scene resembled a stock-car race.

Goods, all headed for the Klondike, were stacked higher than a man's head in Seattle.

Steetcar tracks, teams of horses and stores specializing in Yukon and Alaska gear were typical of downtown Seattle after the strike in the Klondike.

There were several voyages that almost became legends during those two mad years. One involved the former mayor of Seattle, W.D. Wood, who became the ex-mayor as soon as he heard of the gold rush. He was in San Francisco at the time, doing whatever it is politicians do while away from their constituents. He immediately wired his resignation to Seattle, then chartered a ship out of San Francisco. His plan was to make a killing hauling passengers and cargo to St. Michael, where they would board a brand-new paddlewheeler for the upriver trip to Dawson City. There was a near mutiny before they even left the dock in San Francisco because Wood had loaded so much cargo of his own to sell in Dawson City that the passengers had no room for either themselves or their gear.

After that was sorted out to everyone's satisfaction (except Wood's), they put to sea for St. Michael. When they arrived, the passengers were in for another unpleasant surprise. The paddlewheeler hadn't been built yet. Yelling "Liar" and "Thief" at Wood, they finally concluded they had no choice but to pitch in and build the brute themselves. They established a tent city on the barren, stormy beach and spent three weeks building the *Seattle*

No. 1, which they nicknamed "The Mukluk" because that is what appeared to have been used as a design pattern.

They got underway up the Yukon several weeks late, and were still 800 miles from Dawson City when the ice caught them. Again they established a city of sorts to sit out the winter. They named their town Suckerville for obvious reasons and proceeded to raid Wood's hoard of food which he had planned to sell in Dawson City. Finally in disgust, and fear for his health and well-being, Wood gave up and fled camp on foot to St. Michael, and passed out of history. The residents of Suckerville survived the winter, performed a wedding, and arrived in Dawson City the following summer.

There were numerous other curious and unusual events, some seemingly bordering on the supernatural. The *Eliza Anderson,* heading north without a compass, first rammed another ship, and then, after surviving a severe storm, ran out of coal off Kodiak Island. They managed to work their way into the protection of a cove, and miraculously found there a rich seam of coal. Later, a stowaway saved the ship from crashing into rocks during a gale. The passengers came to believe he was a messenger from heaven, or wherever it was that stampeders got their assistance.

But the queen of the fleet was the 191-foot *Portland,* which started the whole ruckus. Like many of the people and other ships in the stampede, the *Portland* had a shadow on her past. She was built in Bath, Maine, and went to sea in 1885 as the *Haytian.* Her owners almost lost her on an early trip to Haiti (then spelled Hayti), delivering a cannon and ammunition to the rebels during the Hippolyte rebellion. The Haitian government seized her but the U.S. government forced her release. Then a gunboat tried to sink her by ramming. She was brought around Cape Horn and used by a Portland, Oregon, firm, supposedly to haul freight, but actually she carried contraband, illegal Chinese aliens and opium. When the smuggling ring was broken up, the *Haytian* was taken by the government, then sold for $16,000 to another firm which gave her the new name of *Portland.* After a few adventures in heavy storms and other near disasters, she was chartered by the North American Transportation & Trading Co., to serve as a link between the firm's Yukon River steamers and Seattle.

It's not surprising, with so many ships heading north along the Inside Passage laden with stampeders and freight, and south with gold, that there should be threats of piracy. The *Portland* owners made quite a splash in the newspapers by arming her with a one-pound cannon (which probably would have been of marginal use at best). But no ships were attacked by pirates during the gold rush. Weather, poor seamanship and lack of maintenance caused enough trouble. There were 8 shipwrecks in 1897 and 34 in 1898. In contrast, in 1896, before the gold rush, there were only three serious wrecks in Alaskan waters.

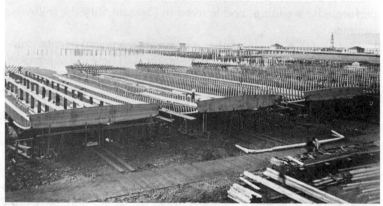

SEATTLE HISTORICAL SOCIETY

With all the opportunity for wealth knocking on Seattle's shop doors beginning that summer and fall of 1897 and continuing on another year, greed became the order of the day. In spite of melodious press releases sent out across the country, there were many transients who preferred the rigors of the passes to the business of getting outfitted and aboard a ship in Seattle.

One can sympathize with the elderly, cantankerous writer, Joaquin Miller, who departed Seattle aboard the *Mexico* on July 26, 1897, on assignment for a magazine. He loudly expressed his pleasure in departing "insane Seattle," only to become a survivor of the *Mexico*'s wreck on August 6 at Dixon Entrance.

Downtown Seattle was, indeed, a busy place. The merchants could hardly keep up with the orders for gear, and warehouse space was at a premium. The more successful shopkeepers gave up and simply stacked nonperishables on the street in front of their establishments. One of the most successful of the time was Cooper & Levy at 104-106 First Avenue South. Years later, Isaac Cooper reminisced about the gold rush and its effect on his business.

It was said that the Moran Bros. shipyard built steamboats by the mile and cut them off at any length desired. Actually, they built only an even dozen during the winter and spring of 1898 for the Yukon River trade.

Within 48 hours of the *Portland's* arrival the city was a bedlam. Money was dug out of safe-deposit boxes and flowed back into circulation. The streets were jammed day and night. In 90 days there came into our store the peoples of nearly every nation; men from Chile, Peru, South America and Australia. Some were grubstaked by friends in the East, spent their money for riotous living in Seattle and never got to the north.

Others got only a short distance from the steamer at Dyea or Skagway, looked at the country over which they would have to make a rugged trail, grew faint-hearted and hurried back.

Queer lines of supplies came into being, everything possible was evaporated to reduce bulk. Plants in Seattle, Portland and San Francisco made evaporated potatoes, reducing 100 pounds to eight to ten pounds, which sold at 20 cents a pound. Onions, evaporated in the same way, sold at 40 to 75 cents a pound. Yolks of eggs were placed in a large vat and by means of a belt turning were changed into a crystal form which sold at $1 a pound. One pound was equivalent to three dozen eggs.

There were other businessmen who sold totally useless items, such as a combination sled and bicycle powered by sail. There were hydraulically compressed bales of hay. Portable stoves that were never tested were offered, along with knockdown buildings, boats and sluice boxes. A compassionate company sold stock in an enterprise to breed and train Arctic gophers to claw holes in the frozen ground and relieve miners of the tedious thawing process! One Thomas Arnold sought capitalization for his Alaska Carrier Pigeon Mail Service Company, which would deliver photographs and messages from the Klondike to Juneau in 24 hours. He wasn't the only one to try carrier pigeons. A *Seattle Post-Intelligencer* reporter named Weston was sent north aboard the *Portland* on its return trip July 23, 1897, with carrier pigeons to send back news dispatches. Newspaper files from the period fail to yield further information on Weston's experiment.

It was a great time for windy prospectors who may or may not have been in the Klondike. But anyone returning from the North could hold an audience spellbound in a Seattle hotel lobby or bar.

One such gentleman, named John J. McKay, told a newspaper reporter there was a dire need for women in the Klondike. "There is but one lady in town who is not married and she has refused every single man in Dawson City. They have knelt before her with uplifted hands full of gold. She wears short skirts, carries an umbrella and wants to vote."

Another veteran of the Klondike, a man named Hall, stopped in Seattle on his way home to Los Angeles and told of the rigors of wintering over in the Klondike.

> "A short time before I left I attended the funeral of Matthew Stacey, an ex-policeman of Tacoma, and A. N. Anderson, both of whom were employed at [Clarence] Berry's camp. They died at the Dawson City hospital. The bodies of both men were strapped to Yukon sleds and hauled to Pioneer Hall, where a party of hardy Yukoners attended the obsequies. A choir, consisting of seven miners and Gold Commissioner Fawcett, rendered music, while at the conclusion of the service we all united in repeating the Lord's Prayer. The burial was as respectable as possible. The bodies were drawn to the hall by six malemute dogs, which cost $2,000. The nails in the coffins cost $8.50 per pound, the wood in the coffins 40 cents per foot, and the work of digging the graves, which occupied six days, cost $200.

"Brain fever," he added, "is troubling many of the people. Men who have been at Dawson for months and are unable to receive word from home worry themselves sick, and in many cases they die. Misfortunes also have much to do in bringing on brain trouble."

The streets of Seattle were almost as crowded and filled with activity as they are today during the annual Seafair parades. Enthusiasts had little red wagons with four to six dogs of various breeds hitched to them, trying to literally whip a dog team into shape before shipping out. Since Seattle almost never has snow on its streets, wagons were the only form of transportation possible for the potential mushers.

Pet dogs were not safe on the loose—the leash law was probably obeyed more rigorously than at any other time in the city's history. There was a man named E. J. Crandall who billed himself as the Dog King of Seattle, and every day during the gold rush he could be found at the lamp post outside the Butler Hotel with a gaggle of yapping, whining dogs he had bought or stolen, trying to sell them to stampeders.

There was also a brisk business in horses to use as pack animals over White and Chilkoot passes. The record of abuse of horses in the history of the Klondike rush is one of the most shameful; more than 2,000—some say as many as 3,000—were worked, starved and beaten to death on White Pass alone. Probably as many or more were killed en route to the passes aboard ship.

One different horse story involved a woman named Mrs. McGuian and her roan horse, Dandy. A stampeder named

Dogs of all breeds and sizes were drafted into service pulling sleds on Seattle's streets, except that the sleds were more often wagons. There were also mining schools where you could presumably learn to pan, sluice or use a rocker.

William Loerpabel came through Seattle to outfit, and Dandy was one of the horses he bought, paying $30 for him. Mrs. McGuian sold the horse because he was such a pest around the house. He ate her flowers, trampled her garden and knew how to open gates and doors. On occasion he was even known to make himself comfortable by climbing the stairs into the house. Mrs. McGuian, tired of his pranks, kept a promise to herself and sold him.

But then she heard of the horrors of White Pass and tried to buy Dandy back. She was angry with him, but she didn't want him brutalized. Loerpabel refused and headed north.

But the story has a happy ending. All the other horses Loerpabel bought were killed in the White Pass area. Dandy survived, and rather than cut him loose to starve or be used by another stampeder, which was the usual thing when a horse couldn't be sold, Loerpabel remembered Mrs. McGuian's pleas. He found a man going back to Seattle and gave him enough

money to pay for Dandy's passage and food, and made the man promise to deliver Dandy to Mrs. McGuian.

He also ordered the man to tell Mrs. McGuian that Dandy had never torn off a pack and never pulled a shoe, that he took everything as it came. Dandy worked hard on the trail and was more sure-footed than the others (Mrs. McGuian, thinking of her stairs, probably agreed). Dandy had become stuck only once when he fell into a deep mudhole. Loerpabel thought it would be Dandy's grave, but since he was now fond of the horse, he hired some men to dig him out.

Armed with the money from Loerpabel, the unnamed escort fed Dandy a diet of biscuits aboard the ship and advertised in newspapers until Mrs. McGuian appeared for a touching reunion. The deep cuts on his legs healed and his diet, presumably including flowers, soon had him fattened up again.

Mining partnerships were formed among Seattle area residents and often a group of men were bankrolled to go to the Klondike with stockholders receiving a percentage of the gains. Businessmen invested heavily in supplies to be shipped up. Among that group was the late Joshua Green who recalled shortly before his death that "there was a lot of money in the Klondike. I know; I sent some up and it never came back."

Newspapermen went up with the intention of starting a free-wheeling newspaper in Dawson City. One of them was Eugene Allen, who worked for Metropolitan Press, a printing firm in Seattle. He and some partners took off late in 1897 with a small printing press, some type and paper. They planned to get the equipment over the passes and down the Yukon River at least as far as Lake Laberge during the winter. The partners knew that Laberge was the first lake to be clear of ice, and if they could be there in the spring of 1898, ready to go, they could probably beat their competition. They did arrive first, but the newspaper business was risky in the boom town, and Allen hardly made expenses.

The famous Oregon Trail veteran, Ezra Meeker, was in his late 60s when the gold rush began, but he loaded up with several crates of chickens and headed north. He made it to Dawson City and sold his chickens at a good profit. Meeker came out again for another load and took them over the passes, too, sold the second batch and then made his single mistake: He invested in mining claims and lost everything. But the legendary western hero left behind a small cabin across the street from the Dawson City post office, which was still standing at this writing.

The streets of Seattle were littered with "steerers," men or boys hired by business firms to steer customers their way. Photographers made fortunes taking pictures of the stampeders standing before their piles of gear before shipping out to the North.

Some of those photographs became part of one of the most successful publicity campaigns in the history of public relations. It was probably the first time that any West Coast city had gone to such trouble to sell itself to the world, and it became something of a textbook program for publicity directors to follow. Nearly all the credit goes to a former newsman named Erastus Brainerd, a salaried huckster perfectly suited as the city's mouthpiece.

Brainerd was a native of Connecticut, a Harvard graduate, and from 1876 to 1880 was curator of engravings at the Boston Museum of Fine Arts. He then went into newspaper work and followed that profession in New York, Philadelphia and Atlanta before getting the westering urge and moving to Washington Territory in 1889, just before it became a state. He was editor-in-chief of the *Seattle-Press Times* and then held the same job on the *Seattle Post-Intelligencer*. In 1893 he became State Land Commissioner and held that office until 1896, when he became Paraguayan Consul in Seattle. He was living there when the *Portland* arrived.

Although the stampeders brought in $325,000 in new business the first month of the stampede—a fortune for businessmen after the long years of the depression—Brainerd felt that there was much more to be attracted by telling potential stampeders that Seattle was the only city to use as a gateway to the Klondike gold fields. He proposed, then founded the Chamber of Commerce's advertising committee, and although his name appeared at the bottom of the list of members, there was never any doubt that it was his committee. It was formed in August 1897, when there was less than two months of good travel weather remaining.

Brainerd gave the committee the official-sounding name, Bureau of Information, and had some letters sent out over the signature of the Secretary of State of Washington State. He said there were three areas of interest the committee should pursue: outfitting the stampeders; getting all the trade that no other city

They were called "variety actresses," but the emphasis must be placed on the word "variety."

attracted; diverting the flow of trade and travel from opposing cities. He added, perhaps a bit self-righteously, that it would all be in the interest of rendering a service to the public.

He worked on getting material to newspapers and periodicals, played on Seattleites' civic pride, printed circulars and correspondence that didn't really look like advertising, and got businesses in town to print letterheads with Klondike slogans and to add, at the end of each letter to inland firms, a sentence or two promoting the Klondike and Seattle.

Brainerd studied his competition—Tacoma, Portland, San Francisco, Vancouver and Victoria—and decided to simply out-advertise them. He bought bigger ads in papers they had already advertised in, and soon Seattle was being promoted in the *New York Journal, American Review of Reviews, Munsey, McClure, Cosmopolitan, Harper's, Century* and *Scribner's*. After it was all over, the records showed that Seattle had advertised five times as much as any other city. Clearly, these publications had good reason to be delighted with the gold rush.

The indefatigable Brainerd had clipping bureaus all over the country busy scanning the printed word for mention of the gold rush and Seattle. When he encountered published comment he thought inaccurate or unfair to Seattle, he would send feature stories or letters to the editor (under someone else's name, the more powerful the better) asking for a correction and at the same time keeping Seattle and Klondike in the news.

He wrote innumerable feature articles about Seattle and the Klondike and released them to newspapers everywhere, and when the *Seattle Post-Intelligencer* published a special Klondike edition in the spring of 1898, Brainerd ordered thousands of extra copies to send around the country. He sent copies to approximately 70,000 postmasters across the nation for them to display in their post offices alongside the wanted posters; about 6,000 went to public libraries; 10,000 copies were sent to the Great Northern Railway for its trains, depots and salesmen, and another 5,000 to the Northern Pacific Railroad.

Not surprisingly, Brainerd found the largest response to his feature stories came from the remaining pockets of poverty, localities that still had not broken out of the depths of the depression.

Then he struck upon what may have been his most effective

campaign of all. He embarked on a word-of-mouth advertising campaign, which any promoter will tell you is the best form of advertising, and the cheapest. He knew that Seattle had a high percentage of newcomers even before the gold rush, and he sent a confidential request to employers and heads of organizations in town asking them to encourage their employees, clients and members to write letters to their hometown newspapers and friends, telling them about the Klondike gold rush. He even asked ministers to suggest this to their congregations. If anyone should happen to be illiterate or awkward with words, "someone" (meaning Brainerd) would be glad to write the letter for them. Naturally this campaign was never announced in print during the period because Brainerd wanted it to appear spontaneous.

We will never know how successful Brainerd's programs really were. Perhaps most of the stampeders would have filtered through Seattle anyway, since it had geography on its side. But there is no record of anyone claiming Brainerd wasted a lot of money.

In an era when truth in advertising—and in news columns—was not at a premium, Brainerd and his committee were surprisingly honest, as this committee report published in the *Seattle Post-Intelligencer* October 13, 1897, shows:

> The Chamber of Commerce of the city of Seattle on August 30 established a bureau of information whose duty it is to give accurate and conservative information as to routes of transportation, cost of outfitting, etc., for the Alaska and Northwestern territory (Klondike) gold fields, and to answer the many questions put by persons desirous of going there. . . .
>
> This committee has prepared the following statement, which is official on behalf of the committee, and is intended to answer in brief the questions most commonly asked them. It is [with some curious spellings of place names] as follows:
>
> Outfit: One man, one year, including groceries, clothing, bedding, hardware, medicine chest and other necessary articles. $125 and upwards. An outfit costing less will be defective in what may be necessary to save life, and at that price food will be

coarse, though it is all that very many take. In this estimate groceries are figured at about $60 for a year's supply, or 16.4 cents a day. A man can live on this, but the best judgement of this committee is that on a proper outfit more should be expended and that what a man should take is all that he needs for comfort and not merely for bare requirements of existence.

Routes from Seattle: a. All water route. Ocean steamer to St. Michael, thence by shallow-draft river steamboats from St. Michael up the Yukon River.

b. By ocean steamer from Seattle to Lynn Canal for Chilkoot, Chilkat and White pass routes, from Dyea and Skagway over the mountains, thence by Lakes Linderman, Bennett, Tagish, Marsh and Le Barge to Lewis river, thence down the Yukon.

c. By ocean steamer from Seattle to Fort Wrangel for Stickeen river route.

d. By ocean steamer from Seattle to Juneau for Taku river route, for Copper river route and for Sushitna route.

e. By ocean steamer to Sitka or Juneau for Kenai peninsula routes.

Note: Routes a and b are the only ones as yet used to any extent. The rest are comparatively unknown, though it is expected that next season their feasibility will be fully proved or disproved, and that steamers will run regularly and directly to each route.

Distances: Seattle to St. Michael, about 2,500 miles; from St. Michael up the Yukon to Dawson City, 1,723 miles. Seattle to Dyea and Skaguay, 834 miles; Dyea to Lake Linderman, 29 miles; Lake Linderman to Dawson City, 841.5 miles.

Time: Seattle to Dawson, by way of St. Michael, between 30 and 40 days.

Seattle to Lynn Canal points, Skaguay and others, 72 hours; Dyea and Skaguay to Dawson average 21 days, more or less according to season, weather and condition of water in river and lakes, assuming that boats, etc., are available.

Seattle to Copper river, 9 days: 6 to Sitka, 2 to mouth of river.

Lines of Transportation: a. To Seattle. Seattle can

be reached direct by the Great Northern railroad, the Northern Pacific railroad and the Canadian Pacific railroad, all of which run their trains into this city, and it is the only city on the coast where three transcontinental railroads do this.

b. From Seattle to St. Michael and Dawson. The North American transportation and Trading Company has its operating headquarters in Seattle, and runs its steamers from Seattle to St. Michael direct, and thus far is the only regular all water route company from Puget Sound.

c. From Seattle to Lynn Canal points. The regular line is that of the Pacific Coast Steamship Company, which has its terminus at Seattle, but during the Klondike rush 63 vessels left Seattle in 68 days for Alaskan ports, more vessels leaving this city than from all other Pacific coast ports put together.

The St. Michael route is open only from about June 10 to September 10.

Note: It is impossible to say how many lines of transportation there will be in the spring. Several local lines have been projected, to say nothing of the many lines projected in the East, nearly every one of which proposes to make Seattle its starting point.

Fares: Fares this year have been $150 to Dawson by way of St. Michael, and $40 first class and $35 second class from Seattle to Lynn Canal points. Spring bookings are now being made at these rates; but doubtless they will be much less in the spring if the projected new lines enter the field. Suffice it to say Seattle will be able to transport all who come.

Fares to the Copper river country are $25 and $40 to Sitka. Thence to Chilkat village, at mouth of Copper river, on Kayak island, $15. Thence to shore by rowboats, $2.00 a day. Fares to Kenai peninsula from Sitka or Juneau from $18.50 to $30.

Cost of Journey: The minimum cost of the journey to the Yukon, excluding railroad fares from the starting point to Seattle will be, on this year's basis, board in Seattle while outfitting—which can be done in less than a day—and waiting for steamer: cost of outfit for scant necessities, say $125: fare to Dyea, $25; freight at $10 per ton, say $6. If a man goes into the Yukon country in the early spring and packs his outfit on a sled he will have nothing to pay except for his dogs in the spring, or his horses in the summer, as the latter are not available for spring use.

Native Indian dogs cost from $75 upwards, and there should be not less than four dogs to a team. Horses cost from $25 upwards. If Indians do the packing the cost is from 15 cents per pound upwards. After the goods are packed over the passes the only other extra expense is for a boat. This year that has run from $100 to $350. The total cost therefore of the

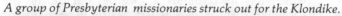

A group of Presbyterian missionaries struck out for the Klondike.

journey, with dogs, horses or packers will be $500 and upwards. If a man undertakes to do all his own packing, which only a man "as strong as a horse" should undertake, he will save the items mentioned.

It is likely, however, that all these items of cost will be lowered somewhat in the spring. No one should start who has less than $500.

Parties: No man should go alone. Not less than two should go together. By forming parties of a dozen or more less supplies can be bought from 10 to 20 per cent cheaper. They will need only one set of camp tools, can pack quicker and make and break camp quicker, and reduce the weight of each one's

LAROCHE

outfit materially. This is a very important point, as the total reduction in expense and wear and tear on persons and packs by going in parties will be found very much less than any one might anticipate, to say nothing of the danger of going alone.

The Best Pass: Questions are asked, which is the best pass? All have their advocates: all have their merits and defects. We believe it is safe to trust the judgement and experience of the Indians. From time immemorial Indians of the coast and of the interior have traded to and fro. They have known of all the passes. They have preferred the Chilkoot pass at Dyea. White men on the whole have done the same. It is the most traveled pass and is certainly likely to be so in the spring of 1898. The other passes, except the White pass, at Skaguay, are practically unknown. The White pass was loudly heralded as the best this year. Many went there. With its difficulties everyone is now familiar. They may exist on the other passes. "Follow the main traveled road" is generally safe advice, and we give it as such for the Chilkoot.

CHAPTER 7
ALTERNATE ROUTES

The Klondike gold rush began with a bang. Within 24 hours of the *Portland*'s arrival in Seattle, men were buying tickets aboard it and other coastal steamers headed north. Outfitters were sending frantic telegrams for more supplies. Farms were mortgaged, pools were formed and straws drawn to see who would take the grubstake and run for the Klondike. Policemen, firemen, streetcar conductors, newspaper reporters, and others quit their jobs on the spur of the moment and headed north. The *Chicago Tribune* accurately called it an exodus, as railroads began price wars and brought the fares from Chicago, Milwaukee and St. Paul to Seattle down to $10. Madames ordered new drapes for their parlors and tickets were sold for rides in passenger balloons from Kalamazoo to the Klondike.

Edmonton, Alberta, advertised the all-Canadian route. San Francisco competed with Portland and Seattle. Vancouver and Victoria appealed to Canadians to depart from there. Everyone was going to the Klondike, it seemed, but the smart money stayed home and sold the stampeders things they needed and things they did not need. Many fortunes were made on the gold rush by people who never, in their entire lives, went farther north than Vancouver.

Chilkoot Pass was the established route to the Yukon from the Inside Passage, but immediately competition from others began. None was as direct, safe or fast as the Chilkoot.

The first and most important competitor was the 2,900-foot White Pass, about which more will be said later.

*It wasn't long before Skagway had an extensive system of wharves out to
deep water.*

WEBSTER & STEVENS

61

Then there was the all-water route from Puget Sound to St. Michael, Alaska, just north of the Yukon estuary. Called the "rich man's route," it was a long way around, about 2,500 miles from the major Puget Sound cities to St. Michael, and another 1,700 miles up the Yukon River to Dawson City. Many who began this trip too late in 1897 did not reach Dawson City before the river froze, and they had to huddle in crude, hastily built cabins through a long winter before continuing their journey.

There were three routes through the Gulf of Alaska: Valdez,

Dyea's Trail Street was appropriately named: It boasted of no boardwalks.

Cook Inlet and Yakutat Bay, and any one was almost as bad as the others.

The Valdez route was over a vast ice field to the Copper River, and up it to a mountain pass and down the Tanana River, which empties into the Yukon. About 3,500 tried this route, at the urging of a steamship company long on sales ability and short on responsibility. Of these, about 200 made the journey. The others either returned to tidewater before it was too late, or went mad on the ice. Several died the slow death from scurvy after suffering the other common ailment of the stampede, snowblindness.

E. A. HEGG

From Cook Inlet another trail led up the Matanuska Valley and over a divide to the Tanana. It wasn't much of an improvement over the Valdez entrance. There were miles and miles of rapids and boulders that tore men's clothing and boots to shreds and reduced many to living off berries. A few who still had money were able to buy new clothing and food from Indians, but it was only a temporary respite until the long winter set in on them with the Yukon not yet reached.

The Yakutat Bay trail was by the worst. Stampeders had to cross the gigantic, crevassed Malaspina Glacier, one of the largest ice fields in the world and not one that sportsmen today tackle frequently. The exact number who tried this route is unknown but there is a record of 100 who struck out across the gleaming, living ice. Only four survived. Theirs was the same fate as the Valdez parties; some froze to death; many went mad and told of giant hairy monsters living far back on the glacier; scurvy rotted their flesh and finally killed them. Of the four who staggered and crawled to the beach a year later, two were totally blind and the other two were nearsighted the rest of their lives.

Farther south, at the tough town of Wrangell, another pitiful route was tried. This one led up the Stikine River to Telegraph Creek, B.C., about 150 miles overland to Teslin Lake. Encouraging men to try this route was no favor. Enough tried it, though, that a detachment of Canadian soldiers, the Yukon Field Force, was sent up the trail to protect Canada's interests in the North and keep it from falling into American hands.

The Ashcroft Trail left from a town of the same name on the great bend of British Columbia's Thompson River. It was heavily advertised as the all-Canadian route by Vancouver and Victoria in an attempt to appeal to national pride. It was one of the worst possible ways to go, but at least 1,500 men and women and 3,000 horses tried it. The trail went up the Fraser River Country and through the Cariboo mining district, the scene of an earlier gold rush, and connected with the Collins Overland Telegraph swath until Teslin Lake was reached. (The telegraph project dated back to 1865 when Western Union sent crews through Canada stringing telegraph cable which was to cross Alaska and go under the Bering Sea into Russia. It was abandoned when the trans-Atlantic cable was successfully laid.)

The record of this trail reads no better than the other alternates.

Suicides, scurvy, horses worked to death, poignant notes nailed to trees . . . The list becomes repetitious.

The worst record of all was established on the Edmonton trails. They were the longest and the most foolhardy, although among the most heavily advertised promotions of the gold rush. In order for stampeders to reach Dawson City by way of Edmonton, they had to undergo hardships beyond belief. They went well beyond Dawson City north of the Arctic Circle and almost to the Arctic Ocean, then swung west and back south to the Klondike gold-fields. In taking this route, stampeders had a choice of going 1,700 miles by way of the Peace River, or down the Mackenzie River system for a total of 2,500 miles more.

They had to navigate that vast inland sea called Great Slave Lake and its sudden, savage storms. They had to track their canoes for hundreds of miles over rapids, slog across miles and miles of muskeg, bogs and windfalls so extensive that one group

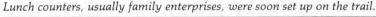

Lunch counters, usually family enterprises, were soon set up on the trail.

By January 1898, Skagway had acquired a permanent appearance.

hacked through 200 miles of fallen forest. Scurvy was as common as mosquito bites, and the trails were dotted with small cabins in which men were left to die the slow, leprosy-like death scurvy offers.

The first survivors of the Edmonton trail arrived in Dawson City in 1899, just in time to see many of its residents heading out to Norton Sound for the black-sand strike at Nome.

So there were only three halfway sensible ways to reach the Klondike: the all-water route and those two passes at the head of Lynn Canal, Chilkoot and White.

It was White Pass that gave Chilkoot the stiffest competition, and eventually stopped Chilkoot traffic dead in its tracks. While the gold rush lasted though, Chilkoot managed to keep a slight edge on White Pass.

CHAPTER 8
SOAPY

Captain Moore may not have been the first to finish a wharf at Skagway, but he did build one and thought he had the town of Mooresville protected against other promoters. In 1895 he helped a group of Californians haul their seven tons of gear over White Pass. They were the first stampeders to use that route. He also cut a trail over the pass and built a small sawmill in anticipation of the rush.

But the stampeders were a particularly ill-mannered lot. Not only did they completely ignore the old man's claim, they also parked their tents and shacks on his homestead and called the new town Skagway, or as some spelled it, Skaguay, Tlingit for "home of the north wind."

Then came the lowest blow: The new town's fathers decided it should be platted. They hired Frank Reid, a stampeder from Sweet Home, Oregon, who knew at least the rudiments of surveying. Like many others on the stampede, Reid had a shadow on his past. He had killed a man in Sweet Home but was cleared on the grounds of self-defense.

When Reid made his survey, one of his streets ran directly through poor Captain Moore's cabin. Moore was ordered to move. Armed with a crowbar, he drove off the first contingent of townspeople, but he knew there was no choice. He bought another lot, probably on his own homestead, and moved there. Then he began a lawsuit that ended four years later when the gold rush was a recent memory. The court awarded him 25 percent of the assessed valuation of the improvements built on his homestead. However, before the judgment was handed down he had improved his financial situation by relocating his wharf and extending it out to deep water.

Very little good could be said of the White Pass Trail until foot

During the early-winter rains, men huddled under shelters wherever they could establish them.

LAROCHE

traffic ended in 1899 and the railroad tracks of the White Pass & Yukon Route reached Lake Bennett. It was torturous for man and beast, impassable at times and the scene of frequent battles over toll roads. Between 2,000 and 3,000 horses were killed on the trail by starvation, abuse and overwork. Epidemics of spinal meningitis were common. Murders, suicides, robberies, con games by the renowned Jefferson Randolph (Soapy) Smith's henchmen were the order of the day. The trail had little to recommend it.

Moore and George A. Brackett both were determined to build a toll road all the way across the trail to Lake Lindeman, where the two trails met. Brackett had the financial backing of such friends as Charles E. Peabody of the Washington & Alaska Steamship Co. to begin his Skagway & Yukon Transportation & Improvement Co., but not enough backing to complete the road, in spite of several important connections in Washington, D.C. Although he had a knack for raising funds at the eleventh hour, Brackett eventually failed and had to sell out to the White Pass & Yukon Route.

Skagway at that time had little to offer in the way of social graces. It was known as a hell hole and visitors became accustomed to gunfire at all hours of the day and night, occasionally having their cabins ventilated by a stray shot. It was virtually ruled by Soapy Smith, about whom millions of words have been written. His curious reign lasted from August 1897, until July 1898.

Like all successful dictators, Soapy was all things to all men. He was courteous to women, kind to children and started a campaign to feed and care for all the stray dogs in town. He contributed generously to churches and itinerate preachers. He was something of a friend to the downtrodden.

He also was a sleight-of-hand artist who parted suckers from their money. He had been chased out of Denver, then the goldfields of Cripple Creek. He had barely escaped execution by the President of Mexico. He was the head of a gang of thieves, murderers and extortionists in Skagway. He ran one of the crookedest saloons and gambling halls in North America. Nobody knows how many widows he created, or how many suicides resulted from his muggings and crooked card games.

In short, he was a fascinating man and by far the most famous character in the gold rush, although he never ventured into the

E. A. HEGG

E. A. Hegg, the famous photographer, captioned this "The favorit [sic] dog team in Sheep Camp."

A team of goats was pressed into packing service.

Yukon River system. He was feared in life, eulogized in death. He, as much as any chamber of commerce effort, made Skagway famous, and today his modest grave outside Skagway is more popular with tourists than the large monument to Reid. Soapy had charisma.

His downfall came at a time in his life when he wanted what no dictator should even think about: Soapy wanted to be loved and respected by the townspeople. He had started the stray-dog campaign and had made it known he was a benevolent, generous man by helping widows and derelicts. He also had taken to drinking heavily when he found his efforts weren't being properly appreciated.

When a horse fell on the trail between Canyon City and Sheep Camp, traffic would sometimes be halted for a half mile behind.

LAROCHE

Then one of his men stole $2,000 in dust and nuggets from a Nanaimo, B.C., prospector named J. D. Stewart. Unlike the Skagway citizens who had been cowed by Soapy and his gang, Stewart loudly and frequently proclaimed that he had been robbed.

A vigilante group that called itself the Committee of 101 swung into action as Skagway's legal guardian because the deputy marshal was on Smith's payroll. While the vigilantes were meeting in a waterfront warehouse, Smith drank heavily and bragged that he, too, had 100 men to back him and that he would get them for a showdown with the vigilantes.

Frank Reid and Soapy had clashed earlier in the day. Reid was unarmed at the time and Soapy told him to go home for his gun. When Reid returned, Soapy was nowhere in sight.

That night Reid, a member of the Committee of 101, was placed on guard with three other men at the Juneau Co. wharf while the vigilantes met inside a warehouse. Soapy, with a derringer up his sleeve, a .45 Colt in his pocket and a .30/.30 Winchester carbine on his shoulder, approached the guards and saw Reid.

"Damn you, Reid, you're at the bottom of all my troubles," he said. "I should have got rid of you three months ago."

There are various versions of the final seconds of Smith's life, but the one undeniable fact is that Soapy was killed almost instantly in an exchange of shots, and Reid was mortally wounded. But he lived nearly 2 weeks, very pleased that he had killed Soapy.

Some think the fatal shot was fired by someone other than Reid. No matter; Soapy was dead, his henchmen were on the run and the Committee of 101 would have their turn at running the town.

CHAPTER 9
THE TRAMWAYS

By the fall of 1897 Dyea had grown from the Healy & Wilson trading post and some 125 Chilkats to a thriving town with out-fitting stores, restaurants, hotels, saloons and a population of about 1,200. A wharf was stretched out into Lynn Canal to deep water, a vast improvement over the conditions faced by early arrivals. They and their goods had had to be lightered ashore, and since the bottom slopes off gently in the inlet, they had to wade the last several feet through sticky mud, occasionally dropping into holes armpit deep. Horses were either swung out into the water on slings or unceremoniously pushed overboard to swim for their lives.

The Chilkats and Sticks were the primary packers during the first few months of the rush, but they were soon faced with competition from men with horses and wagons, then the vastly more modern aerial tramways.

Lumber was sold in Dyea at a premium and the supply was always limited. Some 1.5 million board feet were imported from sawmills around Southeast Alaska and Puget Sound. Corrugated tin roofing was sold at a great markup. Dyea was a genuine boomtown and soon had streets laid out (although no record of its plat has been found). Seven aldermen, a treasurer and a clerk were elected by February, 1898.

Late that spring the population was almost 4,000. The town had frame saloons, log cafes, gambling parlors, stores and real-estate offices. Competition had reduced the price of lodging and meals to 25 cents each. It was a buyers' market.

Dyea had other factors in its favor. It was the traditional and familiar route to the Yukon; its record as a decent place to visit hadn't been besmirched by the likes of Soapy Smith; it had a chamber of commerce that sent a "live wire" representative to the Puget Sound cities and to Victoria and Vancouver to drum up trade. Not the least important asset was the system of aerial tramways, some in operation by early winter with more planned for completion by spring.

By early autumn there was a horse-powered tramway from The Scales to the summit, but it wasn't as ambitious or functional as the others to follow. Archie Burns, a prospector who had been through the Circle City and Fortymile rushes, installed the first engine-powered hoist at Chilkoot early in December. He had a gasoline engine at the summit, a pulley drum and about 1,500 feet of cable with a rope long enough to reach the foot of the pass. Burns hitched sleds to the cable, cranked up his engine and for 2 cents a pound hauled the sleds to the summit by winding the

Once the tramways were in operation, the Chilkoot climb became more of a hike for those who could afford the freight.

cable around the drum. But that winter Burns left and some cold stampeder burned the wooden drum to keep warm.

Soon there were other tramways, each more elaborate and efficient than the last. By the spring of 1898 there were three serving the pass. The Alaska Railway & Transportation Co. started its tramway 2 miles above Sheep Camp. A bucket model, it was on poles relatively close to the ground, and like Burns's rig, powered by gasoline rather than steam.

Next was the Dyea-Klondike Transportation Co.'s bucket tramway at The Scales with a capacity of 500 pounds to a bucket. It had a minimum of supports and in one spot the buckets swung wildly 300 feet above the ground. The firm charged 5 cents a pound.

The most expensive, longest and the last to go into service was the Chilkoot Railroad & Transportation Co.'s professionally surveyed and built tram. Financed by Tacoma men, the area was surveyed by A. Mel Hawks of Tacoma in September, 1897. He and his backers were particularly interested in the stretch between

E. A. HEGG

Sheep Camp and Crater Lake. After his survey was completed and he reported back to the Tacoma financiers, they decided to make it even more extensive.

In October, Britton Gray of Tacoma filed articles of incorporation to construct a tramway all the way from Dyea to Crater Lake, and farther north if needed. They hired Hugh C. Wallace as construction superintendent, a man who later became the U.S. Ambassador to France.

Soon after he began work, Wallace found it would be too expensive and time consuming to build it all the way to Dyea. With wagons using the stream bed in the summer, and the ice and snow in the winter, he reasoned it better to begin the tramway at Canyon City, although he left open the possibility of a horse-powered tramway from Canyon City to Dyea.

Construction was begun on December 10, 1897, but little was accomplished before March because of the unusually heavy winter snow. The tramway had two loops, the first 4 miles long from Canyon City to Sheep Camp and the other over the pass and

Tramway supports were under construction before winter, 1897, in Canyon City.

The Chilkoot Railway &
Transportation Co. began its
tramway at Canyon City.

down to Crater Lake, 4¼ miles long. The trolley automatically switched from one cable loop to the other at the junction and each load was limited to 400 pounds, in boxes measuring 40x20x24 inches.

The entire system was engineered carefully with an eye for both safety and efficiency. The buckets were moved by a light, endless line called a traction rope, which traveled continuously on terminal sheaves, or grooved wheels, which still lie beside the trail in places. The system was called the "double rope" as opposed to the single-rope system in which one rope serves both as support and power.

The tramway had another unusual feature, and perhaps an engineering first. Other systems had used "locked-coil" cable because the outer wires interlocked with each other to create a smooth surface and were flexible enough to be shipped in coils of 800 and 2,400-foot lengths. Special couplings made a smooth splice.

Because of the high cost of transportation, the CR&T ordered "smooth-coil" cable, which is composed of numerous round wires wound in a single strand ⅝ inch in diameter. They were of crucible, or plow, steel for strength and had an ultimate weight of

36,000 pounds. The major disadvantage was that should a cable break, it could unravel for hundreds of feet.

Wallace and his crew laid out the line of tract cables and erected tripod-shaped supports with enough weight between them to prevent the cable from rising out of the channeled, or grooved wheels. There were spans up to 1,600 feet between high ridges with no support. Buckets with a Webber Grip, pointed levers that bit into the cable to avoid slippage, were used.

In addition to the tripod-shaped main supports, sections of iron pipe were bolted together and embedded into rocks, with cross timbers similar to utility-pole crossarms attached to them. Some of these still stand on Long Hill beside the marked trail.

When the tramway opened in May, 1898, the stampede was waning but still moving. The tramway's customers were met at the long wharf by a CR&T agent, who arranged to load their gear onto wagons. The wagons hauled the gear upriver to Canyon City at ¼ to ½ cent a pound. There, the tramway took over and hauled the gear on to Crater Lake for 7½ cents a pound.

Everyone was happy about the tramways except the Indians. They found some work on the Canadian side between Crater Lake and Lake Lindeman, although ferries and wagons cut into their

The Klondike Transportation Co.'s powerhouse was at the crest of Long Hill.

business there, too. But no longer could they bargain against the tramway rates, then strike for more money at The Scales, a favorite ploy before the tramways were built.

Shortly after the CR&T tramway opened, the other trams joined forces with the newcomer. At one point plans were made to dismantle the shorter tramways and use them to extend the Canyon City-Crater Lake service all the way down to Lake Lindeman. The plan failed to materialize, as did the dream of putting both Skagway and the White Pass toll road out of business entirely.

The tramway partnership set a common rate of 10 cents a pound for through traffic, but there were frequent long delays with goods piled up at Canyon City. The machinery wasn't perfect and breakdowns were common. There were also the usual charges of favoritism, often justified when a large shipment came in. The smaller shipments had to wait.

CHAPTER 10
THE REINDEER FIASCO

By November of 1897 the stampede beyond the lakes had ceased. With the exception of a handful of experienced prospectors with dog teams, the traffic down the Yukon stopped when the lakes and rivers froze. From then until the following June, stampede was a cruel way to describe the activity along the trail to the Klondike. Coastal steamers and the hastily reconverted, resurrected and repaired ships still disgorged passengers, freight and animals at Skagway and Dyea wharves, and traffic on the two passes continued. But it was slow traffic with a short, cold destination.

The only thing the stampeders could do to while away the winter was haul their gear from tidewater to the boatbuilding towns of Lindeman City and Bennett. Many couldn't afford the tramway rates, nor could they afford to sit idle for 4 or 5 months in midwinter waiting for spring thaw. Many began the torturous business of packing their gear over the pass only to give up after one or two trips, then sell out at a great loss and leave for home. Only the hardy or the desperate were there at spring breakup.

In the meantime, Dawson City had too much of a good thing. It was a boom town, perhaps the greatest in the history of North America. But it couldn't support itself. Gold lost its value that winter as millionaires and the destitute faced a common threat— starvation. The old-timers on the Yukon were taking good care of themselves and had brought enough food to survive the winter, but not the newcomers who got through before the Mounties

Indians, whites, women and children served as packers if the price was right. This is one of the few summer photos taken during the stampede.

enforced minimum requirements. They came only with their dreams of instant and abundant wealth, and it seldom occurred to them they should also bring food.

By autumn it was apparent to the traders there would be a famine that winter, and they and the steamboat companies urged those without claims or a winter's food supply to leave on the riverboats before the freeze hit. Many did, but not enough. Those who took the last boats downriver toward St. Michael were caught in the shallow water or ice and sat out the winter far from civilization. They were forced to spend months listening to the wind and the groaning, cracking ice on the river.

Others stayed in Dawson City and had it equally rough. While the old Arctic hands knew enough about nutrition to drink an occasional cup of spruce-needle tea to prevent scurvy, many did not. Some of the claim-stakers worked throughout the winter beneath the pall of lung-clogging smoke as holes were fired in the desperate digging for bedrock and its colors.

They were likely to suffer from scurvy, in part through ignorance but largely because they were so intent on reaching gold that they did not bother to eat properly. Some showed up in Dawson City only when the first telltale signs of the disease appeared—general lassitude, loose teeth, bruiselike marks on their bodies. It was a suffering that could have been avoided, but they considered it a calculated risk.

The story of the starvation winter of 1897-98 soon reached the Outside, and the Puget Sound cities that had helped spawn the gold rush began taking action. Fearing the bad news of the starvation would damage business in the spring and summer of 1898, the cities, chambers of commerce and congressional delegations demanded relief action. In December 1897, Congress appropriated $200,000 to purchase a herd of reindeer, of all things, to send to the Klondike and avert the famine.

The Klondike Relief Expedition (also called the Yukon Relief Expedition) was one of the strangest occurrences during a strange time. A delegation went to Norway and bought 539 head of reindeer from Laplanders, shipped them to New York and hauled them across the continent in cattle cars. The animals were then loaded on steamers bound for Haines Mission where they were to be driven up Jack Dalton's trail. With this odd, zoo-like retinue were 43 Laplanders, 10 Finns and 15 Norwegians, whose colorful costumes delighted the publicity-conscious Puget Sound cities.

In the meantime, George A. Brackett, the White Pass toll-road builder, had told his friend, Senator C. K. Davis, that the situation was not serious at all. "Miners who have been there many years say there is more provisions there per capita than they have had in years gone by," he said. "But people demand luxuries." He did concede that prices were unusually high for some items. Bacon, for example, was selling at a dollar a pound.

But Congress had acted and the Klondike Relief Expedition would go through. In addition to the reindeer, which were bought at the insistence of the famous Alaska missionary, Rev. Sheldon Jackson, 150 tons of supplies were shipped to Dyea aboard the Steamer *George W. Elder* and stored at Healy & Wilson's warehouse until the packtrain to haul it arrived. Another

Looking out of place and overdressed, the Lapp herdsmen with their colorful clothes and exotic hats made a striking sight on the streets of Seattle as they waited for orders to head north, long after the starvation winter was over.

shipment arrived toward the end of February aboard the *Oregon*, along with a detachment of soldiers. Capt. David L. Brainerd was in charge and he had 2 other officers, 22 packers and 101 mules. Seventeen of the packers were civilians and five were black soldiers of the 9th Cavalry.

The expedition settled in at Dyea and waited for the reindeer to arrive before heading for the Klondike. By this time, however, Secretary of War Russell A. Alger had decided to abandon the project. Not only was he convinced it was never needed, he knew it could save no lives at that late date even if it did go in. Supplies from regular sources would arrive at about the same time the relief expedition did, or sooner. Consequently, he asked Congress for permission to dispose of the supplies, including the reindeer. Congress approved part of the request, but knowing well the influence of Sheldon Jackson, one of the most powerful men in the North at that time, the reindeer were ordered sent on to the goldfields. On April 19, 1898, the provisions were sold at public auction in Dyea.

The reindeer didn't arrive until May, and they were sent to Haines Mission and over the Dalton Trail rather than down the traditional route. The poor reindeer and herders fought swamps, swift streams, vast snowfields and glaciers. Reindeer died by the score. Wolves and Indians killed some for a taste of new meat. Others strangled on their own harness. Most casualties were from starvation.

On January 27, 1899, the remaining 114 reindeer and the herdsmen arrived in Dawson City. The Klondike Relief Expedition had arrived but nobody cared. Many had forgotten about it and others had never heard of it until they saw the exotic animals straggling down the street. Behind them was a group of men and women dressed in strange costumes speaking foreign languages.

"Nothing surprised us anymore," recalled one sourdough. "None of us had ever seen a reindeer before, let alone a Laplander.

"But when you think about all the other crazy things that happened those two years, we kind of figured it was part of the program."

CHAPTER 11
CHILKOOT WINTER

Life was harsh that winter of 1897-98 on Chilkoot Pass. For nearly 8 months—from October until June—the population grew in Dyea, Canyon City, Sheep Camp, Pleasant Camp, Lindeman City and Bennett. Smaller way stations had opened between the established tent cities to sell meals, liquor, women and gear abandoned by stampeders. Arizona Charlie Meadows, who later built the fine Palace Grand Theatre in Dawson City sold liquor by the shot at The Scales. Another small settlement appeared at the southern end of Long Lake. Ironically named Happy Camp, it remained small because the wood supply was limited. Other cabins appeared all along the Canadian side of the trail as packers, teamsters, ferry operators and cafe owners set up businesses.

Many veterans of the trail later wrote books about their experiences, or kept diaries that were preserved. These personal accounts tell the story of the Chilkoot better than any after-the-fact historian can.

One of the earliest accounts was written by Arthur Treadwell Walden, an adventurous young man who went to the North and worked for several years as a dog-team driver. He made his first trip over the pass in April 1897, before the gold rush struck.

He rode from Juneau to Dyea aboard a small tug and wrote:

> The trip was about one hundred miles up the Lynn Canal and very rough. We had to seek shelter for several hours until the gale blew itself out.

Almost everyone was seasick and lay around on the covered deck, cold and miserable. I remember one large and very sick man who was lying on his back with his head toward me. My collie Shirley, whom I had brought from home, was lying beside me, and for some unknown reason he got up, walked over to this man, scratched his hat off and with the other paw raked the whole length of his bald head. The yell the man let out raised the whole boat and sent Shirley back to my side, where he lay down as before. The man seemed to think it was all part of the seasickness and, as he was large and powerful, I did not care to enlighten him.

Dyea was the last town on the coast, at the mouth of a small stream called the Dyea River, and at the beginning of the Chilkoot Trail. The town consisted of a trading post run by Heron & Wilson [Sam Herron was manager of Healy & Wilson's at this time, not owner—*Ed.*] and a dozen or more Indian shacks. Here our tug anchored about a mile out, at the head of Lynn Canal and our outfits were put on a lighter which was warped in-shore. There was a good deal of floating ice which complicated matters. When there were horses to unload, they were backed over the side and made to swim ashore.

The beach and the country for half a mile back were destitute of snow, and as we depended on snow

By midwinter, instant "towns" had sprung up along the trail.

for our sleds, we had to have our outfits hauled across to the snow line by a pirate horse team which took our last dollar. There we made our first camp in Alaska, along with about a hundred other men who were getting their provisions up the trail by repeated "back tripping" or relays.

On April 1st we left the coast for our journey into the interior. The real work of getting into the Yukon began here, and each man, unless he was rich enough to hire someone to carry his outfit over the lakes at the headwaters of the Yukon, was absolutely dependent on himself. The Indians were charging one cent per pound per mile for packing, and were not overly eager to work, even at that price.

Walden gleefully told of one party from the East who tried packing their own gear over, but soon tired of it and attempted to bargain with the Indians. After a few minutes of haggling, one Indian called the party's leader a "cultus Boston," jargon for "no-good American." The white man was immensely pleased and told a friend that "even the unsophisticated aborigines recognized us as cultivated Boston people."

Walden commented that this party never reached the summit, and that about the only people who had their goods packed over the pass then were traders and gamblers.

Since most of the people on the pass in the spring of 1897 were seasoned sourdoughs or at least knew the life in the Yukon, several had a 7-foot-long by 16-inch-wide Yukon sled and pack-straps. Already the practice of teaming up with another man was common—one to guard supplies while the other packed a load up to the next cache.

"A lone man, if he could get along at all, certainly had the best of it," Walden said, "although I have known men who could not even get along with themselves." He added that three partners was usually one too many, and some diaries bear this out by telling of men afraid to fall asleep at night for fear their partners would rob or desert them.

When he reached the area where Canyon City would be built within a few months, Walden had to go over a series of frozen waterfalls and in some places had to build pole bridges similar to ladders. The river had frozen while the water was still high, then as it receded it took some of the ice with it, leaving gaping holes several feet deep to the bottom layer. It was a risky business, crawling over the top layer.

The summit climb itself was so steep, he said, that a man "standing in the footholds cut in the hard snow could touch the wall in front of him without losing his balance."

The method of getting horses over the summit couldn't have endeared the stampeders to the S.P.C.A. Walden said horses were fastened in a rope sling and led up the trail by a long rope to the summit, "with 100 men or more on each horse until the horses lost their footing, when they were hauled up to the summit lying on their sides. They were then led through the sharp cut [of the summit itself] blindfolded, backed over the edge and slid down the other slope on their backs to Crater Lake. . . . This was not as rough as it sounds, and was the only way of getting them over. I did not see a horse that was either hurt or frightened, but then they were Western ponies." One event on the trip that made a deep impression on Walden was the death of a dog. During an unusually cold night a man driving a team made up of the usual long-haired dogs with one short-haired greyhound, left them all outside that night. The next morning the greyhound was found standing outside, tail tucked between his legs, his back arched and head down. He was frozen solid in his tracks.

"There were some short-haired dogs on the trail, but men were always careful to let them sleep in their tents," he said.

It took Walden and his partner 23 days to get their 1,200 pounds of gear from tidewater to "Lake Linderman" (as he spelled it). Rather than stopping at Lindeman or Bennett, Walden and his partner went on down the lakes to Tagish Lake, where they built their boat and waited for spring thaw, well ahead of the stampede. Like many others, Walden didn't become wealthy on the gold rush, but he managed to have a lot of fun.

That winter, Sgt. William Yannert of the 8th Cavalry was sent over the trail to reconnoiter and map the two passes for the Klondike Relief Expedition. He left Dyea alone on February 28, 1898, with a handsled and 200 pounds of gear. The frozen Taiya River served as a broad highway up to Canyon City, which at that time had 30 cabins. The valley narrowed down to a "gulch of only sufficient width to pass one man or wagon at a time," he reported. The grade steepened considerably for the next 2 miles beyond Canyon City, then leveled off again before Sheep Camp was reached at the head of "a narrow and level valley."

He spent his first night at Sheep Camp which had a transient population of between 350 and 400.

On March 2, Yannert struck out for the summit and saw a large number of other men on the trail. He said the climb from Sheep Camp to The Scales was harder than any other stretch of the trail, including the summit climb.

"The ascent is by no means a gradual one," he reported to his commanding officer, "but consists of a series of steep inclines utterly impossible to surmount without ice creepers, especially if one is hampered by a pack or sled."

It took him 10½ hours to reach The Scales, and he said that if he had to make the trip again, he would prefer to pack his gear rather than pull it on a sled.

Burns's hoist was operating from The Scales to the summit but Yannert avoided paying the 2 cents a pound Burns charged and took the Petterson Trail. By that time, the 1,500-odd steps of the Golden Stairs were well worn and a rope had been stretched on the right side of the steps for packers to hold onto. A deep furrow was worn beside the steps by men sliding down the steep slope, which Yannert said took barely 5 minutes compared with the

There were a few level spots above Sheep Camp, but very few.

45 minutes or more required to climb the stairs. It took Yannert four trips to get his outfit to the summit.

He made his last descent over the Petterson Trail, or Gap, to the right of the stairs. He said it was longer, not as steep, but "worse than the other as it does not offer a direct downward course."

After his gear was safely on the summit and had been examined by the Royal North-West Mounted Police, Yannert headed for Lake Lindeman. He made the steep, 400-foot trip down to Crater Lake by guiding his sled from behind with ropes. The trail from Crater Lake to the foot of Deep Lake led across the frozen surfaces of three lakes and their outlets, making the hike considerably easier than in the summer.

There were two trails from Deep Lake. One was called the Canyon Road and followed the river's course down the frozen rapids to Lake Lindeman. The other, the Hill Trail, paralleled the canyon and came out near the Canyon Road. The Canyon Road was preferred by those with dog and hand sleds, Yannert said, and the other by packers.

A small settlement, again consisting mainly of transients, had been established at Lake Lindeman, along with some sawmills and boatwrights. Yannert was held up there 2 days by a storm and stayed with two Mounties guarding a cache of goods. On March 5, the weather cleared and he went on down to Lake

LAROCHE

Bennett, where the other RNWMP post with 20 men was built at the mouth of the short stream connecting the lakes.

One of the most distinguished women to cross the Chilkoot during the rush was Martha Louise Purdy, the wife of William Purdy of Lake Geneva, Wisconsin. A native of Chicago, she was then 32 years old. In Seattle her husband changed his mind about joining the stampede, but she and a brother rode the *Utopia* from

Long Hill, below the summit climb, deserved its name.

Seattle to Skagway. After a stop at Skagway about July 1 to unload cargo the ship continued a couple of days later to Dyea. Mrs. Purdy watched the *Utopia* steam away with considerable misgiving about her decision to join the stampede.

The Purdy party left Dyea on July 12, 1898, with the men carrying 60- to 80-pound packs. Other stampeders had horses, oxen, milk cows, goats, dogs and burros pulling vehicles of every conceivable description. The Purdys had enough money to hire packers to carry their several tons of gear for $900 in cash.

E. A. HEGG

On clear days, Long Hill looked as if an army was invading it.

About midafternoon the first day they stopped in a trailside cafe at Finnegans Point for a brief rest and ham sandwiches washed down with tea. By this time Finnegan and his two sons had abandoned their attempts to collect tolls over a corduroy road they built in a bog, but their name stuck at the turn in the river.

Mrs. Purdy saw scores of dead horses beside the trail above Canyon City, and they looked inside an abandoned cabin and saw a ruined, mildewed outfit left behind. They were told it belonged to two brothers who died the previous winter from exposure.

They spent the night in Sheep Camp and Mrs. Purdy stayed in the Grand Pacific Hotel, which reminded her more of her parents' woodshed than a hotel. She received the only private room the hotel had to offer—a cubicle partitioned off with a low wall. It had a built-in bunk filled with hay and two old Army blankets for covers. To her pleasant surprise, there also was a feather pillow. For this and two meals, the hotel charged $1. (She didn't comment on one feature of another hotel that baffles people; it was built with one corner over a stream. Perhaps it advertised running water.)

While making the climb up Long Hill, Mrs. Purdy deeply regretted having to wear the costume of the day—high buckram collar, tight corset, long corduroy skirt and full bloomers, all of which seemed to hamper her every step.

When she was near the summit, she slipped and tumbled into a crevice, cutting her leg. She couldn't hold off any longer. She sat down and cried.

Every man who passed offered to help her. Her brother, growing impatient, cried, "For God's sake, Polly, buck up and be a man. Have some style and move on!"

This infuriated her, so she got up and marched grimly to the summit and straight into an ancient tent that served as a cafe. She was very cold, tired and sore and asked for a fire. The owner told her wood was 25 cents a pound at the summit.

"All right, all right," said her much-concerned brother, "I'll be a sport. Give her a $5 fire."

After the $5 fire died down, the party continued—to the customs station, where she saw her first Mountie. "A finer, sturdier, more intelligent-looking man would be hard to find," she noted.

Their party made the hike down to Happy Camp with no difficulties and ate a $2 supper of ham and eggs, bean soup, prunes, half-cooked bread and butter.

The summit climb, directly above the tents, is more intimidating without snow covering the rock wall.

When the snow stopped, the area around The Scales and the summit was a mass of scrambling humanity.

Some appeared to hang onto ledges along the summit by their fingernails.

The toughest part of the hike for her was the last 2 miles to Lake Lindeman from Deep Lake. (Everyone had his or her favorite rough spot.) The trail they took led through a scrub pine forest and they tripped over bare roots of trees "that curled over and around rocks and boulders like great devil fishes." Her brother carried her most of the last mile, and another member of the party hurried ahead to get a room for her at the Tacoma Hotel. Her bed that night was a canvas stretched on four logs with a straw "shakedown." After building a boat, the party reached Dawson in early August.

Mrs. Purdy later divorced her husband and married George Black, who became Commissioner of Yukon Territory, a M.P. and Speaker of the House of Commons. Mrs. Black also served as a M.P.

All during that winter goods were lugged over the summit on men's backs, up the Golden Stairs from The Scales below. The packers dug turnouts into the snow every 20 steps with room for up to half a dozen to pull out and rest at a time, leaning against the slope without having to take their packs off. Boats were packed across (an entire steamboat, the *A. J. Goddard*, was taken over White Pass, a piece at a time), and sawmills bound for the lakes, cookstoves (one was kept stoked by its owner, a widow, as she pulled it down the trail), dogs were carried over on men's backs because they couldn't navigate the steps, and freight wagons piece by piece to use between Crater and Long lakes.

Crude, engine-driven sleds and other useless but imaginative inventions were usually abandoned by the time the summit was reached, and hikers today find many items along the trail they are unable to identify or explain. One of the most perplexing piles of artifacts is the cache of nearly 200 knockdown, canvas-covered canoes up on the rocks east of the summit gap. Were they left because the owner arrived too late to sell them at a profit, or were they simply useless and part of some con-man's goods, or did the owner die? It is unlikely we will ever know.

Gradually, as the snow deepened, the pile of goods at the summit and just below it on the Canadian side began growing in layers until by spring thaw there were at least seven separate layers of supplies, each marked by poles stuck into the snow. But the 70 feet of snow that winter buried the poles, too, and the owners had to burrow down in the approximate location of their cache.

Not all the gear was dead weight. Some took crates of live turkeys and chickens, and one man had a batch of kittens to sell as pets to lonely prospectors and dance-hall girls who wanted something to love.

Saloon keepers rigged up kerosene cans with false bottoms to get liquor past the Mounties. Others hid jugs in bales of hay and cotton or in egg crates between layers of eggs. Dance-hall girls' skimpy costumes were protected from mildew and tears in soldered cans. The Hills Brothers of San Francisco had a monopoly on coffee because they were the first to have vacuum-packed coffee, and it was in 20-pound solder-top cans.

One man's food supply for a year read something like this: 400 pounds of flour; 50 pounds of cornmeal; 50 pounds of oatmeal; 35 pounds of rice; 100 pounds of beans; 40 pounds of candles; 100 pounds of sugar; 8 pounds of baking soda; 200 pounds of bacon; 36 pounds of yeast cakes; 15 pounds of salt; 1 pound of pepper; 1/4 pound of ginger; 1/2 pound of mustard; 25 pounds of evaporated apples; 25 pounds of evaporated peaches; 25 pounds of evaporated apricots; 25 pounds of fish; 10 pounds of pitted plums; 50 pounds of evaporated onions; 50 pounds of evaporated potatoes; 24 pounds of coffee; 5 pounds of tea; 4 dozen cans of condensed milk; 5 bars of laundry soap; 60 boxes of matches; 15 pounds of soup vegetables and 25 cans of butter.

Add to this a small metal stove, a gold pan, granite buckets, cup, plate, silverware, frying pan, coffee pot, pick, saws, whetstone, hatchet, shovels, files, drawknife, axes, chisels, nails, sled, rope, pitch and oakum and a canvas tent. He also had to have several changes of clothes and those suitable for a country with a 150-degree range in temperature; mosquito nets, bedding, a small medicine kit and other items of equal importance.

By the end of that crazy September the trail was strewn with unnecessary gear bought by the unwary from merchants on Puget Sound and in Dyea. Revolvers were found beside the muddy path, heavy stoves and useless mining equipment, trunks abandoned in favor of packboards made of sticks, wheelbarrows, scraps of harness and articles of clothing deemed unnecessary weight.

Worse yet was the human suffering along the trail. Injuries were common and doctors few and far away. There were uncounted murders, more than contemporary accounts would imply, and usually over theft. Sometimes murders were committed over matters as important as poorly cooked beans. Women accompanying their husbands were sometimes seen sitting and sobbing beside the trail as men turned their heads in embarrassment and walked on past. There were suicides, a few only partially successful.

There were many cases of snowblindness. Pneumonia was

Many college students worked their way north as packers.

frequent. There were epidemics of spinal meningitis that turned an already miserable situation into a day-long nightmare. Not only was everyone afraid of the disease, they had to listen to the stricken men and women screaming with pain for a few hours— 2 days at the most—until they were silenced forever. Some were buried in snow beside the trail without benefit of clergy, only to appear bloated in the spring.

The problem of health and medical care was made apparent

early, and Dr. I. H. Moore of Seattle went to Skagway early in the winter to do what he could to fight epidemics of spinal meningitis, smallpox and other diseases that swept the passes and threatened the entire stampede. He fought the epidemics all that winter and founded the Bishop Rowe Hospital in Skagway, where he treated the men and women who became ill and struggled back to town.

Not all made it back to town. One man lay crumpled, moaning in the snow for hours with a broken leg while the steady line of stampeders inched past him, ignoring his pleas for help. Then, toward the end of day, a professional packer headed back to tidewater came by, picked him up and carried him to Dyea.

Foolish old Joaquin Miller, the "Bard of the Sierras," had written it was little more than an elegant wilderness hike. A few months later the Mounties in Dawson City asked him to leave town because his numerous stories in newspapers and magazines were misleading tenderfeet into believing the North was something like a park in downtown Cleveland. The pity is that they didn't turn him back at the passes. The poor, silly old man simply could not believe what he saw around him, and convinced himself he was seeing an epic performed before his eyes where everyone was happy and nobody got hurt. This despite a close brush with death himself.

There were other examples of inhumanity, of men discarding the veneer of civilization with other belongings that seemed inappropriate to the Chilkoot. There were hundreds of pack animals simply turned loose when they could go no farther, and the gaunt, bloody horses and burros would wander through camps and the makeshift towns looking for food or a soothing hand. Arthur Treadwell Walden told of his partner going back to the summit from Crater Lake, then down to The Scales, with a rifle to kill the abandoned, starving animals until he ran out of ammunition, then returning to the tent and going to bed without saying a word.

Personal cleanliness wasn't so much a fetish at the turn of the century as it is now, but even by those standards, men became pretty rank. They went for weeks without changing clothes, and were unable to wash and dry their socks. After wearing a pair of socks a few weeks in those high, laced boots so popular then, a man could take them off and hardly recognize what he found at the end of his legs. If he was lucky, he would find a pair of awful-smelling feet; if unlucky, he would find them infected, swollen and rotting.

There were miners' trials along the trail, usually for theft. At the funeral of one thief, who had committed suicide rather than submit to punishment, an itinerant preacher delivered a brief, impassioned eulogy and ended the service with these words: "He that maketh haste to be rich shall not be unpunished." It struck some bystanders as an obvious but rather cheeky thing to tell a group of people brought there by a common greed.

The 19th century was an age of diaries and journals, and many men on the stampede were aware they were participants in a unique historical event. Many were anxious to set down their adventures while the scenes were still fresh in their memories. Keeping diaries in the dead of winter on the trail must have been difficult: hands numb from the cold, the paper wet from storms and perspiration, and fatigue that became a way of life.

A young man from Seattle, William M. Schooley, kept one of the more enlightening and complete diaries. He discussed hardships as matter-of-factly as entries in a weather report. He repeated the rumors that swept up and down the trail, and his entries often reflected the competition and an almost civic pride that grew up on both passes. The reading material he mentioned was typical of the stampede; it, like the event the young man participated in, was highly romantic and adventurous. Scott, Stevenson and Kipling were best sellers on the trail.

Schooley began his diary shortly after he and his friends—whom he never completely identified—landed at Dyea with their provisions and dog team:

JANUARY 30—Canyon City, Alaska. We moved the first load of our outfit from Dyea today and have it moved to this place now. We hauled from 800 to 1,000 pounds with our six dogs. Met a man who had his feet badly frozen on the summit yesterday.

JANUARY 31—Sheep Camp. We brought our first load here yesterday and got permission to camp on a lot near the trail. We shoveled away about four feet of snow for a place to put our tent. The wind is blowing terribly hard.

FEBRUARY 1—Lafe got up this morning to cook breakfast and found that the stove pipe had been carried away. He found the pipe and we had to cut one of the joints to make it fit tight. Last night and this forenoon was the windiest weather I ever spent in a tent. The flapping of the tent would catch the pipe and jerk the stove so that we could hardly cook. I looked for the tent to blow down any minute but by 2 o'clock the wind had abated some. Lafe cooked some oatmeal mush and tallow for the dogs, and Frank and I shoveled away the snow for our tent in a sheltered place in the timber about 400 yards from here. We will move there tomorrow, thank heaven.

FEBRUARY 2—Today we moved to the timber and have the most comfortable camp we have had during our Alaska rounds. Ours is a 10 by 12 tent. The bed is spread in the back on about one foot of hemlock boughs. Frank put a puncheon floor in the front half. This evening we dug a hole in a snowdrift near the tent for the dog house and covered it with a tarpaulin and boughs. The dogs have about as comfortable quarters as ourselves now. Last night we let them sleep in the tent with us, it was so cold. It is reported that some Indians came down from the summit today badly frozen and others of the same party were lost and perhaps perished.

FEBRUARY 3—Today we broke the dog team and each of us took two dogs and brought a load from the Canyon. We got a late start and back to camp early with 500 pounds apiece. The dogs work fine. We met a party of about twenty Indians today on the trail. They belonged to the Stikine tribe and were coming down to Dyea for provisions. They crossed the summit yesterday but got off the trail near the Stone House. It was storming hard and all of them but one squaw, a little 8-year-old boy and a little babe, branched out to find the trail again. They found the trail but lost the ones they left behind. They made their report at Sheep Camp and some white men went in search of the missing. They found the squaw and little boy frozen to death, but when the mother saw she must die she put her own clothes on the little babe and it was found alive and warm. Just one other showing of a mother's love. About 90 people landed at Dyea today. I think the rush is on in earnest. Several women came up the trail today.

FEBRUARY 4—This was a fine day down here, but storming above the Stone House. Sledding was good. We brought up 2,600 pounds from the canyon. Even now much time is lost in passing people on the trail. I think the blockade will show first in the canyon. The report came that three men froze their faces near The Scales today. There is danger on and near the summit. One man took a slide down The Scales yesterday with a pack on his back and was badly injured. Three men froze to death on Skagway Trail yesterday. Every man on the trail seems to be pretty good-natured except now and then when the dogs do not "mush on" properly.

FEBRUARY 5—Lafe is on the sick list. Frank and I took three dogs apiece and brought in the last of the outfit from the canyon. We brought about 1,500 pounds in two trips through the canyon. We feed the dogs all they will eat every evening after the day's work is over. It looked bad to hitch them up without any breakfast, but experienced dog teamsters say that is the proper way. We find that the wind blows through these woolen mackinaws, so Frank or I will perhaps make a trip to Dyea tomorrow to get parkas to wear over them and to get the mail.

FEBRUARY 6—Dyea. I came to Dyea this morning from Sheep Camp. A north wind has been blowing all day, making it disagreeable for those sledding up the trail, still it is only 8 degrees above zero. The trail is icy and the two dogs brought me down in a hurry. Good sport if I was alone. I left an order with the tailor to make us three duck parkas tonight. They will cost $12, a pretty stiff price when we are so near bedrock. Two yarn caps, some tallow and a few cooking utensils are the rest of my purchases.

FEBRUARY 8—Today is cloudy. It was snowing and blowing so bad above Sheep Camp that we did not sled. This morning I read "The Man in Black," by Weyman. I did not like it much. I am reading now "Twenty Years After," by Dumas. We have eight or ten volumes of fiction that Keasby sent to Lafe which will help us to pass away the time we cannot sled. Packing is down to three-fourth of a cent now from

Dyea to Sheep Camp. The packers here combine as well as farmers.

FEBRUARY 9—Lafe and I took 150 pounds each to the foot of The Scales. This afternoon Frank and I took another 200 to The Scales. We made our cache on a high point of rock that the wind would sweep the snow away. Some of the fellows have their outfits deep under the snow and cannot find them. An almost unbroken line of men, horses and dogs reached from Sheep Camp to the summit. All sorts of contrivances for moving the grub was used. Those who have not dogs, horses, oxen or an elk prefer to pack their stuff from here. One lady on the trail is helping her husband to pack over. Day before yesterday an old man about 60 had both of his legs broken while going up The Scales. Some man turned his sled loose at the top and in coming down it crippled the old man. It is reported that some goods were stolen at the summit.

FEBRUARY 10—We moved 750 pounds to The Scales today. Sledding is good and the trail was lined with men. Getting provisions over Chilkoot Pass is a hard proposition. In December last about 1,000 pounds of provisions were stolen from a cache six miles from Dyea. Today the thieves were caught with the goods near the summit and brought to Sheep Camp. A committee was elected this evening and the trial was held in a tent saloon. The men were brought in one at a time to testify and their testimony was conflicting. There were three in the party. One of them saw that he would be convicted, so he fired a shot at one of the guards and ran down the trail toward Canyon City. Excitement ran pretty high. A party started after him, but it was unnecessary; he had committed suicide after running a short distance by firing a bullet through his head. His body was brought back to the saloon for people to look at and the trial proceeded. The committee returned the verdict that one of the remaining two was guilty of stealing, and that the other was innocent. The people then voted that the innocent one should be free after doing what he could to show the goods to the owner, and that the accused should be tied to the stake tomorrow noon and let those who desire lash him.

He is to be branded a thief with paint and chased out of the country. I saw enough of mob law to turn me against it. The people mean well enough, but are governed pretty much by feeling.

FEBRUARY 11—We landed another 750 pounds at The Scales today and I am pretty tired. I hear that another outfit of goods was stolen from the summit last night. A meeting was announced tonight to organize a vigilance committee to provide means for preventing thiefs and punishing same. The man convicted last night was stripped to the waist, lashed to a post and whipped today. The whip was a piece of new rope tied to a handle and he was lashed seventeen times. He yelled considerable and remarked he would rather be hanged, but after it was over he walked down the trail towards Dyea before the guards with the words, "A thief, send him on," above him, with a pipe in his mouth and a smile on his face. I do not think the shame of the thing pains such a character. He was made to leave the country last year for the same offense.

FEBRUARY 16—We took 750 pounds more to the foot of The Scales. It was pretty cold. Lafe frosted his nose and ears a little. A man here posts letters for 5 cents each and he also brings mail from Dyea if a name is left with him. This evening I began reading "Louise de la Valliere," by Dumas.

FEBRUARY 17—We took one load apiece, 450 pounds, to The Scales. It was quite cold. Frank had his nose frosted a little. Most every one wore masks and it resembled a procession of culprits. One man froze to death on the summit last night.

FEBRUARY 24—Lafe went to Dyea today. It was blowing so that we could not work above here, so I laid in camp and read "Dr. Rameau," by George Ohnet. A man died here yesterday and another is not expected to live long. Eighteen men died in the last week at Skagway from the same spinal disease. It looks pretty risky. The doctors do not understand.

FEBRUARY 28—The English flag floats on the summit now, meaning they will collect duty there. So many people are on the trail now that it looks like the main street of a crowded city.

MARCH 11—Frank and I took loads to The Scales

for Tom Naw for which we received $16. I read some in "The Master of Ballantrae" this evening. A man was shot on the Skagway trail through the back and robbed.

MARCH 12—We worked all day on the summit and made a showing. The blockade was bad. One had to stand a half hour with pack on his back before he could work into the line and then had to go very slow.

MARCH 14—We put the last of our outfit on the summit. Two fights occurred at The Scales. There are many cranks on the trail. One man shot his partner this morning above the heart and he will probably die. The shooting was brought about in dividing the grub.

MARCH 17—Three cables are in operation up The Scales. Sold 100 pounds of bacon on the summit for $20.

MARCH 21—We camp tonight on the shores of Bennett, about 14 miles down. Brought the last of our goods to Lindeman.

MAY 2—We went on the hill and sawed a log containing seven boards 15 feet long, 1½ inches thick and 12 inches wide for the ends of our scow.

MAY 3—We sawed a log today containing six boards 7 inches wide, 1 thick and 26 feet long for the top sideboards of the scow. Papers are selling for 25 cents each. Our talk is nothing but war and patriots are coming to the front.

MAY 8—We saw a paper of April 1 containing an account of the Manila naval battle. How good it makes one feel.

MAY 20—We finished pitching the boat. It is 16 feet long on the bottom and 26 feet long on top with a six-foot beam. It will weigh about 1,500 pounds.

MAY 28—Anchor Point, between Bennett and Tagish. We left about 10 o'clock, having covered about 16 miles. A great fleet of boats and scows are tied up here on account of the ice. I estimate the number at five hundred. It is reported that fifteen boats were smashed up in the ice at Tagish. A man from New York was knocked into Lake Bennett by the boom and drowned.

> *MAY 30*—The fleet was augmented by a few hundred more boats today. For a mile boats are tied up along the beach thick as can be.
>
> *JUNE 16*—About 9 we came to Dawson.

The Chilkoot Trail was truly an international settlement. There were people from nearly every nation in the Western Hemisphere and a few from the Far East. At times it was something of a Tower of Babel as the people included Maoris from New Zealand, former slaves from the American South, taciturn cowboys from Texas, Swedes, Norwegians, Germans, Swiss, South African Boers, South Americans, Australians, and prostitutes from each ethnic group.

There were tourists from New Zealand and the British Isles. Remittance men from Western Canada went to escape boredom. Teenagers were taken along and used as work animals by desperate relatives. Mattie Silks, Denver's most famous and successful madam, took eight girls over the pass and down to Dawson City. Missionaries went in hopes men would remember they had souls. College athletes quit school and some worked as packers to finance their sabbatical. Lawyers from New York City tucked their shingles under their arms and hiked the trail.

Only on Ellis Island in the New York harbor could a census taker have found such a complete cross-section of humanity.

Chapter 12
IRON MAN STEELE

Although John J. Healy's popularity didn't rise when he called for legal help back in 1894 on the Yukon, he inadvertently did both Canada and the stampeders a great favor. That initial Mountie force of 20 enlisted men and two officers had been sufficient to maintain peace and collect customs before the stampede. But not after July 1897. The surgeon of the force, Dr. Wills, the first permanent doctor in the Yukon, had an area the size of France as his medical domain, and he couldn't possibly tend the sick when his patient list could conceivably grow to 100,000 within a year.

In October 1896, the Royal North-West Mounted Police established a post at Tagish Lake to collect customs. In June 1897, another detachment of 19 men headed by Inspector W. H. Scarth joined the existing force headed by Inspector Charles Constantine. The reinforcements hiked over Chilkoot Pass, and during the first week of August another group of Mounties arrived in Skagway. They tramped up to White Pass and established the customs post at that summit.

In addition to collecting customs, their arrival also served notice to the United States that Canada intended to draw the boundary line across the crest of the Coast Range.

The Mounties announced they would levy a duty of "about 20 per cent valuation on all goods going in [to Canada], whether for speculation or necessity." They also would enforce a rule requiring roughly 1,150 pounds of food per person, and certain other necessities for surviving a year in the Yukon. However, they said they would not be strict with men already en route, but would enforce both regulations without fail on newcomers.

Soon the Mounties had stations at every practical route to the Yukon, and it was rare that a party slipped past them without being seen, although many tried. About the only record of anyone entering without paying customs or being checked are those who waited until the Mounties closed shop during a blizzard. The risk would seem hardly worth it.

In addition to the Mounties, the Canadian government sent other officials to the area. Thomas Fawcett was gold commissioner and D. W. Dean was sent as collector of customs. Fawcett, however, became unpopular and was suspected of accepting bribes (a charge never proven). He was removed and replaced by that Yukon old-timer, William Ogilvie, whose reputation for fairness and devotion to duty was unsurpassed. Major J. M. Walsh, a veteran Mountie, was named first commissioner of the newly-created Yukon Territory.

Walsh went by ship from Vancouver to Skagway and arrived on October 8, 1897. With him were 10 constables, a dog driver, 100 Mackenzie River huskies and Inspector Zachary Wood, grandson of former President Zachary Taylor. In the same party were Clifford Sifton, Minister of the Interior, Justice McGuire of the Northwest Territories Supreme Court, a secretary and a legal aide.

At no time in the history of the gold rush did the United States send as many powerful politicians to protect its interests in the Territory of Alaska, but it was Canada that was being inundated by citizens of another country. She had more to lose than the United States, and indeed, she did—gold exported to this country, and the boundary settlement that gave her no exit to the sea.

Combining an inspection tour with their trip to Dawson City, the party hiked over Chilkoot and stopped briefly at the small Lake Bennett post that had been established by Inspector Harper. When they reached Tagish post, they found that the men there were stopping vessels, collecting customs and numbering vessels as they passed. The names and addresses of each occupant were recorded, a practice that became a major bookkeeping chore during the stampede. But it eliminated the uncertainty in case of accident, and enabled the police to account for every boat and occupant on arrival in Dawson City.

111

Each man was checked as he crossed into Canada to see if he had the 1,150 pounds of food required.

Three months later still more Mounties arrived at Skagway. This detachment of 22 men, nine dog drivers and 43 packhorses landed on January 7, 1898. It was led by Inspector Robert Belcher. His superior officer, Wood, told him to take over at tidewater and Wood headed down the Yukon to Big Salmon, where Major Walsh's party and a group of prospectors were detained by an ice jam.

The Wood party had a rough time on White Pass. A series of storms struck the party and they almost lost several packhorses because the snow was so deep in places they nearly smothered. For a week the temperature hung at 40 below. They pushed on to Lake Lebarge where they met the Walsh party. Walsh and his group had given up reaching Dawson City and were returning to the coast.

Then, on February 14, 1898, Samuel B. Steele, who was to become a legend, arrived in Skagway. He had sailed up on the small but seaworthy *Thistle*, which had been used in the fur-seal trade.

"My berth was one of three situated above the screw, in a little cabin which had a strong odour of ancient cheese," he wrote. "The berths were so small that it was with the greatest difficulty that we could remain in them when the boat pitched in the heavy seas which she encountered during the voyage.

"The master of the vessel and his pilot were natives of Newfoundland, skilled in navigating the icy seas in the whaling and sealing industries, and no better sailors than they are can be found. The food was coarse but well served, and, as there were more than 200 to feed in the little vessel, only 120 feet in length, the tables were crowded all day, only one-sixth of the passengers being seated at one time."

It was 30 degrees below zero when he stepped off the vessel on the Skagway wharf, and the north wind was roaring down the Skagway River Canyon off White Pass and "searching us to the bone," he said.

Two days after Steele's arrival, Inspector Wood returned from his cold perch in the mountains and told Steele he had posted parties at each pass "to establish the *true* boundary and guard the passes" [italics added]. Wood said each station was provisioned for 6 months, that the men were quartered in tents and that cabins were under construction at each pass which would serve as customs stations and quarters for the officer in charge. He also said each station was equipped with a Maxim gun and "sufficient" ammunition.

The Maxim, one of the original machine guns, was single-barreled and water-cooled. The matter of having heavily armed Canadians at the summit of the Coast Range raised a howl of protest from the Skagway and Dyea citizens that was heard eventually in Washington, D.C.

The treaty still hadn't been settled and the Canadians once had tried to post a customs officer in Skagway because she considered it and Dyea ports of entry into the Yukon. But the Americans were singularly uncooperative to the lonely customs collector and he was withdrawn.

Canada split the difference. The United States claimed territory down to the lakes; Canada claimed to saltwater. So when the Canadians withdrew from tidewater, they stopped at the summits

Boats, sleds, cookstoves, sawmills and spare socks were among the items packed up the Golden Stairs that mad winter.

CANTWELL

of the passes, safe in their assumption that the climate was too rigorous for American bureaucrats.

It was Steele's duty to guarantee that Canada's border began at the passes, and he came armed with a set of orders from Ottawa to protect not only the national boundaries but also the matter of customs and gold being shipped back out of Canada. His first inspection trip was to Chilkoot Pass and it got off to a poor start when several members of his party slipped on the ice covering the Dyea wharf and fell into the inlet. Their lives were saved but they had to traipse on into Dyea with injured dignity and frozen uniforms.

On February 22, Steele and Inspector Skirving started for the summit, traveling with several teams and wagons hired from the companies that built the tramways. They fought their way through a savage blizzard, often crouching behind the wagons, and had to spend the night at Canyon City in the tramway company's stables.

It was still storming the next morning, but they pushed on for the summit. At Sheep Camp they passed a group of prospectors, as Steele wrote:

> . . . many staggering blindly along, with heavy loads on their backs, some of them off the trail and groping for it with their feet. These we assisted to find it, or they would have most likely have fallen into the numerous holes along the trail.
>
> When we arrived at the foot of the steep ascent from a point called The Scales to the summit, the storm made it impossible for us to find the lifeline which had been placed to guide the people up the steps cut in the ice which covered that part of the ascent, and we turned back to the camp of the men who were constructing the tramway.
>
> It was difficult to find, and we had almost given up the search when Skirving called out, "Here it is, sir!" and there I found a tunnel which led into a huge snow drift which covered two large tents. One was occupied by the civil engineers, the other by the laborers, cooks, etc., of the company and two men were busy shoveling the snow out of the tunnel to prevent the occupants of the tents from being suffocated.

The storm was still blowing the following day, and Steele borrowed the tramway company's telegraph system to tell Superintendent Perry back in Dyea the reason for his delay. A few minutes later, a corporal named Pringle came down from the summit to report that Inspector Belcher's party was ready to begin collecting customs and inspect stampeders' belongings. Steele sent the corporal back with instructions to begin collections the next day. He forwarded his baggage to Lake Bennett, where he would have his headquarters. Content to know the Union Jack was flying on the summit, he returned to Dyea.

> On our way down to Dyea the weather changed for the better, and many thousands of men were on the trail, packing their supplies to the summit, or in caches near The Scales at the foot of the big hill. The work of these men was very severe, each one having to bring into the Yukon district at least 1,150 pounds of solid food besides tents, cooking utensils, prospectors' and carpenters' tools or he would not be permitted to enter the country. Money was of little use to him, it could purchase nothing, and starvation was certain if no food were brought in.
>
> This order given by the commissioner of the territory was one of the wisest given in the Yukon, and was the means of preventing much trouble and privation; needless to say it was strictly enforced.

Steele did not like Skagway.

> The population increased every day; gambling hells, dance halls, and variety theatres were in full swing. "Soapy" Smith, a bad man and his gang of about 150 ruffians ran the town and did what they pleased; almost the only persons safe from them were the members of our force. Robbery and murder were daily occurrences; many people came here with money, and next morning had not enough to get a meal, having been robbed or cheated out of their last cent. Shots were exchanged on the streets in broad daylight, and enraged Klondykers pursued the scoundrels of Soapy Smith's gang to get even with them.
>
> At night the crash of bands, shouts of "Murder!"

cries for help mingled with the cracked voices of the singers in the variety halls; and the wily "box rushers" [variety actresses] cheated the tenderfeet and unwary travelers, inducing them to stand treat, twenty-five per cent of the cost of which went into their pockets. In the dance hall the girl with the straw-coloured hair tripped the light fantastic to a dollar a set, and in the White Pass above the town the shell game expert plied his trade and occasionally

Viewed from the side, the summit climb appears dreamlike, a frigid vision of hell.

some poor fellow was found lying lifeless on his sled where he had sat down to rest, the powder marks on his back and his pockets inside out.

He spoke more kindly of Dyea but didn't think much of Sheep Camp:

Many thousands of men and some women were encamped there [Sheep Camp], most of them engaged in packing their supplies over the summit, all anxious to get to the headwaters of the Yukon to build their boats for the passage down. Neither law

CANTWELL

nor order prevailed, honest persons had no protection from the gangs of rascals who plied their nefarious trade. Might was right; murder, robbery, and petty thefts were common occurrences.

He told of one Sunday morning when he and Wood were roused from their sleep in Skagway by a gunfight outside their house. "Bullets came through the thin boards, but the circumstance was such a common event that we did not even rise from our beds. Wood jocularly suggested that we should get up and take a hand in the scrap, but that was all."

While a few Mounties took advantage of their positions and

Still they came, amid snowstorms, and the Mounties were there waiting for them at the summit.

E. A. HEGG

staked rich claims on the creeks outside Dawson City, those working on the passes suffered as much or more than any of the stampeders. They had to sit out blizzard after blizzard and extremely low temperatures while stampeders headed for the protection of timber at Sheep Camp. Their quarters at the summit were impossible to heat properly and the enlisted men took turns standing watch to keep the fire going.

During one of the worst storms, the Mounties on Chilkoot were forced to abandon the summit and move down to the frozen surface of Crater Lake. But that night the water level rose in the lake and flooded their tents, getting their sleeping gear wet. They pulled sleds into the tents and spent the rest of the night on them.

They brought their firewood up from the Canadian side, which meant a 7-mile walk for the men detailed to the job, and many were badly frostbitten when they returned. Wood was closer on the south side of the pass, but Americans would surely have complained about it, all the way to the nation's capital if necessary.

Snow fell constantly that winter, 70 feet deep at the summit according to some accounts. Everything the Mounties owned was constantly wet and mildew attacked their papers. From February 25 to March 3 the weather was dry and cold for a change, but another storm struck and continued with only an occasional pause until May 1. On one day during the worst of the storm, several feet of snow fell and the Mounties continually shoveled it away from the tents and Inspector Belcher's shack so they wouldn't suffocate.

Although White Pass is lower than Chilkoot, its summit area is longer and flatter, and timber is farther away. Logs for the Mounties' buildings had to be hauled 12 miles by horses, but the Union Jack was raised on February 27 and customs collection began. The first buildings were built on the ice and Inspector Strickland suffered most of the winter from a serious case of bronchitis. Steele relieved him briefly, but he, too, suffered the same affliction.

Steele's men collected thousands of dollars a day during the height of the rush because the goods were purchased outside Canada. "Had the miners outfitted themselves at Victoria or Vancouver they would have saved themselves a large amount of money," he observed. However, those who did purchase their supplies in Canada had to ship them under seal to the passes or pay duty in Skagway and Dyea to the American collectors. They couldn't win, although customs posts were not established at the port cities until well into the stampede.

Steele's passion for order was frequently tried by antics on the American side of the passes, and it is no credit to the Americans that the Canadian side was superbly managed and foul play was almost unheard of. On one of Steele's many trips over the Chilkoot to Lake Bennett, he told of seeing thousands of people in one day, like a laborious ant hill.

> The gamblers and shell game ruffians were busy taking what they could out of the numerous tenderfeet who were on their way in. Like the majority of their kind, they thought they "knew it all" until they found themselves minus most of their dollars, and realizing the situation, began to fire their ill-aimed revolvers at the expert, who occasionally got impatient at the fusillade and returned the fire with fatal effect.

Steele blamed Soapy Smith for everything of this nature on the trails, although it is doubtful that every scalawag on the stampede worked for him. Steele also deplored the lack of honor among thieves.

> The previous week one of them on his way down the Chilkoot to Dyea, with 900 dollars in his pockets, the proceeds of his day's work, sat down to rest. He wore spectacles and, as he gazed pensively at the snow, one of his own sort came along, poked his gun under his cap peak, demanding, "Cough up your pile, or I'll blow your specs off!" He coughed up both pile and pistol, and was told to "git" which he made haste to do.

Steele flatly stated that there was no danger of Soapy and his gang on the Canadian side of the passes. "They would not show their faces in the Yukon."

During the winter Steele established his headquarters at the mouth of the stream that leads from Lake Lindeman to Lake Bennett because that was the busiest point and the end of the trail.

A strange city grew at the summit as gear was cached everywhere.

Both the White Pass and Chilkoot trails terminated there and a combination tent and wooden-shack city grew rapidly around the north end of the lake where the timber supply was best. The stampeders began building a church on the hill overlooking the lake, and it still stands today as the men left it when the ice broke, the outer shell completed but the interior bare of floors and other amenities.

After Steele set up his headquarters, he seldom had an opportunity to leave his combination office and living quarters. He rose each day at 4 or 5 A.M. and usually worked until 10 P.M. or midnight. He dispensed information on the Yukon and

And when it snowed, most of the gear was covered, leaving only poles to mark it.

ASAHEL CURTIS

Klondike, settled disputes, and oversaw the census taking and boat registrations.

> All sorts and conditions appeared to consult us as to what they could or should do, and amongst them were men and women who had been doctors, lawyers, clergymen, soldiers and engineers, and women in tights—by far the most convenient dress for them—all hurrying along the trails to the new Bonanza.
>
> Deaths were brought to our notice occasionally, and then we took hold, acted as administrators, kept a careful count of everything in possession of the deceased, disposed of the effects to the best advantage, except watches and trinkets which might be prized by the next-of-kin and mailed them to the proper address.

The Mounties under Steele's command were a gentlemanly sort, the kind made famous in movies a few decades later. On one occasion a young couple on their honeymoon were going over White Pass after sending everything but a small valise ahead by pack train. They broke through the ice and were soaked to the skin. A Mountie placed his tent and wardrobe at their disposal, and the young bride rode on to Bennett wearing his scarlet jacket and yellow-striped pantaloons.

One of the few people to amuse Steele that winter was America's "poet scout," Captain Jack Crawford. "Cap'n Jack" was one of the West's great characters and one of America's worst poets and dramatists. He wrote epics in both literary forms that are interesting today only for their length, inferiority and childish charm. But Crawford was lovable, harmless and decidedly entertaining.

Intending to put the stampede on a paying basis, Crawford brought along four tons of machinery for his gold-washing operation. He checked in Seattle and found his food and other essentials could be purchased in Dyea and Skagway for about the same price—except for bacon, crystallised eggs, condensed food and hardware—after deducting the price he would have to pay for freighting the goods up there. To his dismay, though, Crawford had to leave his dredge behind because it was too heavy for the tramways. Some of its components weighed 700 pounds each, 300 pounds over the limit.

He rode the *Brixham* and arrived at Skagway on April 19, 1898, 2 weeks after Chilkoot Pass's worst avalanche. He had been warned against the Chilkoot because of the avalanche and went ashore in Skagway to haggle with freighters. The lowest quote he could get was 13 cents a pound. Too high, he fumed, and went over to Dyea.

There, the DKT Co. told him his gear could be moved from tidewater to Crater Lake for 10 cents a pound. Pleased, but still a bargainer, Crawford said they could have his business for 9 cents a pound. The DKT agent accepted, and guaranteed delivery in 9 days. Then the agent phoned the superintendent in Canyon City and told him of the deal. When the superintendent heard Crawford had 13,000 pounds, he went one better. He guaranteed delivery in 8 days.

"Make the contract," Crawford ordered.

He stayed in Dyea until April 24 to purchase groceries and other supplies. Then, early that Sunday morning he and two other men—a Dr. Wilcoxen and J. Crook—started out on horseback for Sheep Camp.

Crawford allowed as how the trail was pretty good, "but owing to the fresh fall of snow, and turning out for packers coming back who warned me that it was dangerous to go on, my horse broke through the soft snow twice, and rolled over."

It happened again and he collided with his horse's head, but he rode on toward the summit after leaving his partners behind in Sheep Camp. He got as far as The Scales before giving up, no mean feat on horseback. The Golden Stairs up the summit were empty of men.

A DKT agent told him his freight, minus his personal baggage, was already at the summit and en route to Lake Bennett by other packers contracted by DKT. This worried Crawford because he didn't think the customs had been paid. So, in spite of the storm that had come up, he decided to head for the summit.

The climb was rough on the old scout and he found the customs house closed due to the storm. The Mounties invited him to stay in the customs house until morning, and since Crawford knew some of them from earlier escapades along the Canada-U.S. border, they treated him to a delicious roast-beef dinner.

The next morning he was told that his freighter had paid a $100 deposit on his outfit, and because everybody knew the poet-scout, his gear was allowed to pass before the complete duty was collected.

At 10 A.M., April 26, just 50 hours after leaving Dyea, Crawford arrived in Steele's office on the shore of Lake Bennett. Steele thoroughly enjoyed his visit because Crawford was a great teller of tales about his old crony, Wild Bill Hickock.

Crawford was quite a showman and used more body English than a slapstick comedian to tell his stories. After he had cut quite a swath in Dawson City, he returned to the United States, wrote some typically wretched historical pageants and toured the continent enthralling, amusing but never boring his audiences.

CHAPTER 13
AVALANCHE

Today as you cross Chilkoot Pass you see two main glaciers above the trail between Sheep Camp and The Scales, both extremely high up on the mountainsides and always appearing on the verge of crumbling and dropping iceberg-size blocks of snow and ice on the valley below. In September 1897, just after the rush began in earnest, the unnamed glacier on Mount Cleveland east of the trail above Long Hill cut loose with a flood.

Apparently, the warm summer had created a large lake in the glacier and the heavy rains on the coast side of the mountains increased its size. Then, early on the morning of September 17, the ice dam holding the lake gave away.

About 25 campers near the gorge at the huge boulder called Stone House heard the roar and had time to dash for high ground. Almost at their heels was a 20-foot wall of water thundering down the vast rockfall toward them. Its force was so great that Stone House was knocked down the trail nearly a quarter of a mile.

When the water struck the gorge, it was deflected down toward Sheep Camp, its force and height weakened by the widening canyon. It ripped up tents in Sheep Camp and swept up several stampeders and washed them downriver. Those on higher ground watched as people grabbed for tree roots and boulders to save themselves and listened to the grinding boulders and pebbles that were rolled downstream by the flood.

When the water subsided, Sheep Camp was a wasteland of scattered tents and gear. Silt, sticks and tree trunks were scattered around the area. Apparently only one man lost his life, although there were unconfirmed reports of other deaths.

The worst natural disaster was yet to come, the Palm Sunday avalanche of 1898. It came after several heavy snowstorms had dumped a deep blanket of snow on the Coast Range. In the last week of March the weather cleared briefly to let traffic continue

At least 60 persons were buried in the Palm Sunday avalanche.

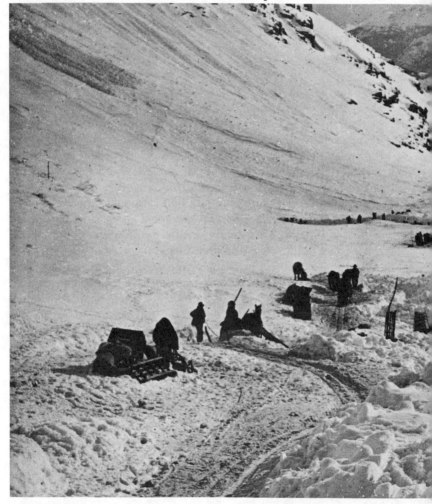

over the pass, but it turned bad again on the 19th with a severe blizzard. Then on the first and second days of April, a warm, strong wind came up from the south.

Veteran sourdoughs knew the danger of soft snow on the steep slopes, and several such as Sam Herron down at Healy & Wilson's in Dyea and the packer, Jack Cavanaugh, warned everyone of avalanches. The Indian packers refused to work at all, but the

E. A. HEGG

stampeders didn't want to waste a good stretch of weather. They kept crawling up the pass.

On that Saturday night, April 2, the owners of a small restaurant at The Scales, Adolph Mueller and Ed Joppe, were kept awake much of the night by a series of small slides rumbling down the slopes.

They were awakened before dawn by a stampeder who told them a family camping nearby had been buried in a slide. Mueller and Joppe pulled on their clothes and helped dig out Mrs. Anne Maxson and two others still alive.

Then they heard another avalanche coming, a much larger one, and roused everyone in the area and told them to make a dash for Sheep Camp. But Mueller, Joppe and several others decided to stick it out at the restaurant.

At about 10:30 that morning the Chilkoot Tramway construction gang abandoned the summit. Without slowing up in their flight they told the others they had better "get the hell out of here and run for your lives. Make for Sheep Camp." They tossed them a length of rope and kept going.

At last Mueller and Joppe decided to leave. But they had waited too long. They ran and stumbled down the trails, carrying shovels in case they didn't make it.

Just as they reached the gorge they heard a roaring noise. Some thought it was a slide. Mueller insisted it was only the wind. He had hardly spoken the words before he was buried to his hips in a vicelike mass of snow rushing down the mountain. He tried to pull himself out but was thrown over on his side and buried in about 6 feet of avalanche.

A man from Maine was directly behind Mueller. He said he heard a loud noise and felt himself moving swiftly down the hill. He saw several others fall, some with feet flailing in the air and heads buried. When he stopped in the ravine he was several feet beneath the silent snow.

Those who survived told similar stories. They were unable to move and breathing was difficult. Many fell asleep during their interment, and those who awoke said they felt refreshed. The others died of suffocation.

Some of the dead were found still in a running position. Others were upside down and clamped by the snow like plaster of paris had been poured over them. Victims could be heard shouting

Volunteers performed the grisly task of digging out the victims.

beneath the snow, their voices growing steadily weaker until they were forever silenced.

And for the second time in one day, Mrs. Anne Maxson was dug out of an avalanche alive.

The construction workers had been missed by the avalanche. They returned immediately to search for the others. An old man stumbled and slid down the mountain to Sheep Camp begging for help. The rescuers dug parallel trenches across the 10-acre slide area, or toward the sound of voices. In some cases the victims' breath created funnel-shaped holes that went to the surface like clam holes on a beach.

One of the romantic stories to come from the passes was that of

The snow was so deep in places that many bodies were never recovered.

Vernie Woodward, a hearty woman packer who was being courted by Joppe. Joppe, presumed dead, was stretched out on the Chilkoot Railroad & Transportation Co.'s powerhouse floor with the other bodies. But he was only knocked unconscious, and Vernie worked on his prone form until midafternoon, giving him artificial respiration, mouth-to-mouth resuscitation, working his arms and legs and calling his name. At last he opened his eyes and spoke her name.

E. A. HEGG

As soon as Steele heard of the slide, he sent a runner from his post up to the summit to tell the Mounties there to assist in every way possible. The customs officer, Inspector Bobby Belcher, organized a committee of "good American citizens" to see that the dead's property was properly taken care of and their names and addresses recorded.

By the time Belcher arrived there were already rumors of looting. But Belcher straightened things out and turned the bodies over to the Dyea citizens for burial. The senior officer of the American Army stationed at Dyea, Col. Thomas Anderson, headed up the trail and found a temporary morgue had been set up at Sheep Camp.

By April 15, some 50 bodies had been recovered and identified, most of which were buried in the Slide Cemetery at Dyea. A few were shipped home at the request of relatives. The total number who died was never known, but estimates have ranged up to 70. By midsummer, when all the snow had melted along the trail, a body would occasionally float to the surface of a pool.

There were other smaller slides that killed people, one the same day as the main one. It hit just below Stone House and killed three men in their tent and covered an ox named Marc Hanna.

Two stampeders from Cascade Locks, Oregon, E.P. Nash and Paul Paulson, bought Marc in Dyea that February for $150 and used him to haul gear up the trail as far as pack animals could go. When he was found two days after the slide, Marc had tramped himself a small cave in the snow and stood calmly chewing his cud until rescuers freed him. He went back to work, hauling bodies down to Dyea.

Another small slide occurred on April 15, seven days after the trail was opened again. Three men were buried just above Stone House, but all were dug out alive within two hours.

CHAPTER 14
THE ARMY ARRIVES

Calls for army support on the trails began arriving in Washington, D.C., soon after the stampede began. Most complaints were concerned with the presence of the Mounties on land Americans believed belonged to their country. One of the first letters was from a commissioner of the Revenue Service stating that a Canadian syndicate controlled White Pass and was collecting a toll of 2 cents a pound on miners' supplies on the United States side of the border. Another revenue official complained that the master of a ship out of Victoria, the *Danube*, refused to show his papers on demand.

A further complaint, which was taken quite seriously by Washington, said the Canadians were cutting American timber in Alaska, then hauling it over the passes to a sawmill on Lake Bennett. Since Washington, D.C., was a long way from Chilkoot, and people "outside" the north were as ignorant of it then as now, the charge was investigated thoroughly. However, it was found that the sawmill was owned by two Americans from Juneau and that they were using Canadian timber near the lake rather than hauling it 7 or 8 miles over the pass.

The mill was an example of the type used during the stampede. Powered by a 5-horsepower steam engine, it had been packed piece by piece to Lake Bennett, and could handle trees only up to 6 inches in diameter. The lumber from it was sold primarily to boat builders at $40 a hundred board feet.

The pressure for military assistance kept growing. The presence of the efficient, fair and remarkably tough Mounties intimidated the Americans and they felt they, too, deserved an army. At last the War Department responded in midwinter, and the matter of the international boundary would soon be settled.

Four companies of the 14th Cavalry at Vancouver Barracks in Washington were sent to the head of Lynn Canal. Companies B and H were billeted at Dyea under the command of Col. Thomas Anderson, and companies A and G led by Lt. Col. George B. Russell were sent to Skagway. Each command had four officers and 108 enlisted men. The battalion boarded the steamer *Undine* at Portland and made frequent stops en route, taking 10 days to reach the Skagway wharves on February 25.

There was immediate need for the army's services. While an officer was ashore reporting to Major Rucker of the belated Klondike Relief Expedition, a brawl broke out on the dock.

The Skagway Ship Co. had begun unloading baggage, using a number of Indians taken aboard at Juneau. Longshoremen attacked them and pushed several off the dock into the frigid

Strings of packhorses were used as far as Sheep Camp, about 13 miles from Dyea.

water. Lt. William D. Conrad, the officer in charge, called out the troops and drove the longshoremen back. Sentries were posted with instructions to protect the Indians while they continued unloading the ship.

The army's first order of business was the matter of the international boundary. Colonel Anderson conducted several interviews with local citizens and learned that the Canadians were well entrenched at the summits of the passes, and that Americans must pay duties on construction materials at the lakes. He also found that several Skagway and Dyea firebrands were trying to form a volunteer militia to drive the Mounties down from their nests on the summits.

Colonel Anderson remained calm and refused to take any action without first consulting his superiors on what could become an explosive situation between the United States and Great Britain. He sent out a feeler to Inspector Steele in the form of a letter demanding to know why the Canadians had been enforcing military and civilian authority in American territory, or at the least in a territory still in dispute. He demanded that these measures be suspended until the boundary question was legally settled.

Steele sent the letter on to Commissioner Walsh, who refused to budge an inch. Colonel Anderson forwarded Walsh's blunt reply to his superiors, and eventually the United States and Great Britain took action to set the boundary. Neither wanted an armed confrontation over territory of marginal political, economic or geographic value.

In August 1898, the International Joint High Commission grew out of this situation, but no decision was reached. The commission did agree to a provisional boundary from near the head of Lynn Canal across Chilkoot and White passes, and a temporary line was marked in 1900.

Finally the boundary question was presented to a tribunal. In spite of Canada's efforts, the tribunal voted against granting her a saltwater exit on Lynn Canal. The deciding vote was registered by a Briton.

When the American Army arrived it took the policy that its role was only to be present. During 1898 there were no occasions when the army's help was needed to keep the peace. Colonel Anderson, with justification, believed his troops could be better employed elsewhere. His superiors at Vancouver Barracks agreed, but decided to keep one company for Skagway and Dyea and recall the others.

Meanwhile, the United States had entered the Spanish-American War and Anderson asked for green troops to replace the seasoned veterans he commanded so the latter could be sent to the tropical battlefields.

About 400 civilians on the passes, or loitering around the towns with nothing to do and no money to take them home, pestered the army to accept them as recruits. Soapy Smith, who hadn't yet tangled with Frank Reid, recruited some of the drifters into a rag-tag army and offered his services as a commanding officer to the American Army. His offer was hastily and respectfully declined. The army thought it could do without enemies both in front of them and behind.

The two companies at Skagway were sent back to Vancouver Barracks, and the portable buildings, horses and other equipment were transferred to Dyea. Colonel Anderson was ordered home

The tramway ended at Crater Lake, left, and horses and mules hauled the goods down to Long Lake.

but was told to stop in Wrangell to investigate reports that the town was in need of peace-keeping services. He did, and found it did. Company H, rather than going home, was stationed at the town with Captain Yeatman in command.

By May 1898, traffic through Skagway and Dyea had dropped considerably. The gold rush was dying.

The tramways on Chilkoot and Brackett's Road on White Pass were insurance against pileups that were customary during the previous winter. Yeatman said an honest judge, C. A. Sehlbrede, had been appointed for the district and that "one honest commissioner and two deputy marshals at each town" were sufficient to keep the peace. He believed his company should be sent to the Spanish-American War, too. His requests were denied.

Shortly afterwards his soldiers were needed down at Pyramid Harbor, then at Skagway. The Pyramid Harbor episode was an attempted murder of Jack Dalton, not a particularly popular man in his time.

Dalton had established the Dalton Trail earlier, and recently had blazed a new cutoff to avoid fording or ferrying the Chilkat

E. A. HEGG

River. The Indians had been earning wages by charging tolls for ferrying goods across the river, and Dalton had dried up that income. So an Indian named Hard Working Jim took a shot at Dalton. Captain Yeatman took some troopers down to settle the dispute, and Hard Working Jim gave himself up.

The troops returned to Dyea only to be called right back because the Indians were threatening the whites. When Yeatman returned he found they had good cause for anger. The Alaska Packing Association, which had been canning salmon there since 1882, had razed a dozen Chilkat houses without paying damages. Also, Dalton's employees had taken over the historic Indian route, the Chilkat Trail, and were charging both Indians and whites tolls for its use.

Yeatman again smoothed things over, then wrote a blistering letter to the Commissioner of Public Lands recommending that land patents not be issued to either the canners or Jack Dalton.

The last major confrontation involving soldiers was the shootout between Soapy Smith and Frank Reid. Judge Sehlbrede called for the army to prevent a mob takeover of Skagway when Soapy fell. A platoon of soldiers stopped the mob and saved a few necks of questionable value, such as Slim Jim Foster, who was within minutes of being the central attraction of a necktie party. The soldiers rounded up Soapy's henchmen and escorted them aboard a steamer bound for territorial headquarters in Sitka for trial.

The soldiers were called on for other minor problems, such as handling the mail when it took 24 hours or more for it to be sent the 9 miles from Skagway to Dyea. They also occupied their time by finding a better site for the post than the edge of Dyea. Yeatman didn't like the first site because water frequently stood for days on the parade grounds, and he knew the hard Alaska winter would make their monotonous life even worse because there was no protection from the wind that whipped down the Taiya Canyon.

He chose a place 3 miles south of Dyea on the west side of the inlet. A military reservation measuring 2 miles long and 1 mile wide was established there. It occupied the Dyea-Klondike Transportation Co. buildings on the dock.

The soldiers were called to settle disputes over Brackett's toll road, and in 1899 stopped a labor dispute when the White Pass &

Yukon Route construction began. Actually, it was more than a labor dispute, it was a small-scale war. The soldiers moved through the streets of Skagway breaking up all meetings between potential troublemakers. Soon the strikers lined up to return to work.

Captain Yeatman was finally relieved in late 1899 after the Spanish-American War was over and the uprising in the Philippines began. The new commander of Vancouver Barracks, Maj. Gen. William R. Shafter, wanted Captain Yeatman and his men back in Washington State.

The replacement unit was Company L of the 24th Infantry, commanded by Capt. Henry W. Hovey. The 24th was one of only four black regular army units in existence. It had a distinguished record since its formation in 1869. It had been on campaigns against the Indians and had fought in the Spanish-American War, losing 38 percent of its force during a two-day battle at Santiago de Cuba. The unit then was sent to Siboney, near Santiago, to guard the yellow-fever hospital there, and when it returned to the States at the war's end, it had lost 300 of 500 officers and men.

When summer came, freighters hauled goods across Crater Lake in canoes.

E. A. HEGG

They left for Alaska on May 3, 1899, and dropped off an officer and 46 enlisted men to relieve the troops stationed at Wrangell. Two days later, on May 20, Captain Hovey and 112 men landed at Dyea to relieve Captain Yeatman of his 15-month tour of duty.

By this time Dyea was a dying town. Its usefulness had ended and it was only a matter of months before it would become a memory. Captain Hovey believed it wouldn't be long before the telephone and mail service would be suspended and recommended that he and his troops be moved over to Skagway. Already, he reported, the sea worms were at work on the Dyea dock piling and he feared it would be completely wrecked in the first winter storm. Before he could wait for an answer, a forest fire took care of the matter for him.

July 28 the troops discovered a fire about 1,000 yards north of the post. They were unable to stop it and called the Pacific Coast Steamship Co. for help. Two ships and several scows arrived and it looked for a while as though they would stop the fire. But a north wind came up and the soldiers had to flee aboard the ships. Five men were left behind as guards, but when the fire started in the moss on the ground, it roared through the post and the guards had to flee in a small boat.

The unit rented a warehouse in Skagway and set up an emergency camp. The next day they saw that the whole face of Halutu Ridge over Taiya Inlet had been blackened.

It was a bad summer for fires, and several broke out in Skagway River Canyon up toward White Pass. The water tank at Glacier Station on the White Pass & Yukon Route was destroyed in one fire, and trains were delayed for hours. One had to dash through a wall of fire and smoke to reach safety.

For the first few days the soldiers were stationed on property belonging to Captain Moore, the town builder, who let them live there free of charge. Later they moved into the Astoria Hotel and were charged $175 a month.

Although there was even less for the black infantrymen to do than the previous soldiers, they remained in Skagway until 1902, when the 106th Company of the Coast Artillery at Fort Lawton in Seattle was sent to relieve them. Apparently the army believed it important to keep soldiers there as long as the Mounties clung to their posts at the summits as they had since 1897.

CHAPTER 15
THE BOATS AT BENNETT

By spring of 1898 the shores of Lakes Bennett and Lindeman were crowded with tents and shacks of every description. The mile-long stream connecting them was lined with shelters and the quiet valley between the high mountains echoed with the sound of timber falling, saws, hammers and men's voices. The spruce was almost depleted in the area as the rush to build boats and have them launched at spring breakup continued.

Sawmills were established, boatwrights were kept busy. Through all this the Mounties roamed, giving instructions to men who had never built a boat in their lives. Rafts, punts, scows, barges, canoes, double-enders, skiffs, junks, catamarans—all were there. Some were purchased already built at prices ranging from $250 to $400. Those who built their own would agree it was a fair price.

For those who did build their own, it was an agonizing ordeal during which numerous friendships and spur-of-the-moment partnerships ended.

The first order of business after setting up camp was the construction of a sawpit. If they were lucky, they could find a spot where four trees grew in a small square or rectangle. These were chopped off about head high and a scaffolding built across the stumps. On this scaffolding the men laid the log to be sawed into rough planks.

One man stood below, the other above. Most whipsaws cut on the downward stroke only and the man below received a face full of sawdust at every stroke. They cursed and sawed and argued

After camp was established came the whipsaw pits so they could build boats.

and fought and stopped speaking. They had survived the test of the passes, but this "Armstrong Mill" was too much for some of them.

Men burst into tears of frustration and rage while working in the sawpits, and others wordlessly flung the saws aside, grabbed half of their gear and never spoke to their partners again. Some partnerships were literally split up, and one pair cut every sack of flour in half rather than sensibly dividing it. Any friendship that could survive both the passes and the sawpits could survive anything.

But the sawing and the hammering and the caulking went on all that winter and spring, until in late May when the boats that would be built were ready for launching. They had been warned of the dangers awaiting them on the run down the river, but they weren't listening. Nothing could be worse than what they had already survived, they said. Nor did the example of John A. Matthews have any effect on them.

Matthews, a young Idaho farmer, tried to navigate the rapids between the lakes the previous summer. After two attempts in

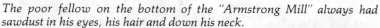

The poor fellow on the bottom of the "Armstrong Mill" always had sawdust in his eyes, his hair and down his neck.

CANTWELL

Those who built boats at Lake Lindeman soon regretted it when they saw the boulder-filled stream they had to navigate to Lake Bennett.

Lake Bennett was probably the busiest small-boat harbor in North America during the spring of 1898.

which his boat foundered and he lost two outfits, he cried, "My God! What will happen to Jane and the babies?" Then he placed a revolver against his head and pulled the trigger.

All along the lakes and all the way down to Carcross the boats were poised on the beaches waiting for the ice to leave. Gradually the mood changed to one of festivity in the tent cities as the weather warmed and the ice kept cracking. Then came May 24 and Queen Victoria's birthday. A holiday was called and the hardened pass veterans took time out to play.

The most popular sport for the occasion was tug of war. There were teams of British, New Zealanders, Nova Scotians, Australians, Scots and Americans. And there was a team of Mounties. True to form, the men in the colorful uniforms to whom the stampeders owed so much, were the victors.

The time of departure was near and the men watched as the slush on the lakes grew softer each day. Snow had long since left the lowlands, and flowers were turning the brown hillsides into an intricate needlepoint.

Before the ice was completely clear, they took their boats out and checked them for leaks.

LAROCHE

And on May 30, 1898, 2 days after the ice cleared, boats were still leaving Lake Bennett bound for Dawson City, the fabled "City of Gold."

Then, on May 29, it happened. The ice broke and began moving slowly to the north toward the Yukon River. Some 800 boats followed the ice out, and the last lap of the race to Dawson City began.

Most waited until the following day when exactly 7,124 boats, 30 million pounds of gear and more than 30,000 men and women set sail for the City of Gold. Many vessels foundered soon after launching because they either hadn't been tested properly, or were overloaded. Some ran aground because the skippers had absolutely no experience in boating. Some found themselves going backward as the almost daily north wind swept down Lake Bennett. Other men, remaining behind to build boats for latecomers, amused themselves by sitting on the rocks and watching the crazy armada shipping water, bumping into each other, spinning crazily and all the other events that are hilarious from the shore and terrifying from the deck.

Little headway was made the first day, and that evening the inland navy was strung out all along Lake Bennett, fires marking the camps after darkness finally fell in the lengthening days. Someone began singing a song. It was picked up by the next

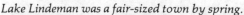

Lake Lindeman was a fair-sized town by spring.

camp, and the next and the next until it was being sung for miles and echoing across the waters to the silent mountains.

On the second day after the ice left, the race continued in earnest and the first of the flotilla arrived in Dawson City on June 8. For the next 2 or 3 weeks the water-borne stampeders rode the swift Yukon down through the rapids, the murderous Miles Canyon, and at last rounded a bend and saw Dawson City and Klondike City (or Lousetown as most called it) on the right bank divided by the magical Klondike River. They caught the eddy created by the Klondike flowing into the Yukon and swung into shore on Front Street to be checked off by the ever-present and ever-caring Mounties.

The stampede was over, but it was little more than an exercise in futility. All the good claims had been staked before they arrived. Only the businessmen among them made any money. Those looking for gold returned home empty-handed. For the rest of their lives, perhaps defensively, they insisted the trip was worth it. If nothing else, it gave them a sense of accomplishment.

CHAPTER 16
RAILROAD BUILDERS

As already indicated, it was the White Pass & Yukon Route that finally ruined Dyea and the tramways, and completely stopped traffic over Chilkoot Pass. Although William Ogilvie had reported that it was possible to build a railroad over White Pass, he said it would be "difficult and costly." Nevertheless, three Victoria businessmen obtained a charter through the Canadian government. When they were unable to obtain financial backing, they sold their franchise to the Close brothers of London in March 1898.

The Close brothers had the money, and set out to lay narrow-gauge tracks where many men said tracks could not be laid. First, they obtained a right of way through the American portion of the route by having five men incorporate a Pacific & Arctic Railway & Navigation Co. in the state of West Virginia. The original plans called for a railroad from Skagway to Fort Selkirk. An extension was requested to stretch the rails on beyond Dawson City to the 141st meridian near Fort Cudahy on the Yukon River.

The Close brothers named Samuel H. Graves of their Chicago office as president of P&AR&NC, who at that time was building a reservoir in Colorado. One of Graves' first jobs was bargaining with George Brackett. It was a tough session because Graves had to pay $100,000 for his toll-road rights at a time when traffic was dwindling.

Surveys were made to establish a route, and construction began on May 27, 1898, with a construction crew of more than 1,000 men, which at times climbed to 1,900. They lost hundreds of men to the

Atlin, B.C., gold rush in August 1898, but most soon returned. The Atlin strike also cost Dyea a few more businessmen, who were convinced it was a dying town.

Track reached the summit of White Pass in February 1899, and on July 6, 1899, it arrived at Bennett. Then on July 29, 1900, construction crews heading south from Whitehorse met those going north from Bennett at Carcross. The usual golden spike was driven—and bent double—by Graves, whose aim with a sledge hammer left much to be desired.

That was the end of Chilkoot Pass. It already had been drained by the Spanish-American War, the gold strike across the mountains at Atlin, the natural death of the stampede after the summer of 1898, and finally the gold rush to Nome in 1899. By the summer of 1899 the boom town was left with only a handful of packers taking whatever business they could find. It wasn't much.

Surprisingly, only one tunnel was blasted through the Coast Range for the White Pass & Yukon Route, a fact that still amazes engineers.

In desperation the tramway owners said they would extend the cable as far north as needed to combat the trains, but the tram cars were limited to 400 pounds of cargo each and could not haul passengers. In a real turnabout, the dying town of Dyea, which so vigorously fought Canadian domination and customs collection 2 years earlier, now petitioned to Congress to have the entire inlet donated to Canada so she would have a seaport and Dyea would have a new chance at survival. Naturally the request was denied.

In 1899 most of the Dyea-Klondike Transportation Co. equipment was torn down and the Alaska Pacific Railroad Co. incorporated its tramway with the Chilkoot Railway & Transportation Co. That winter the White Pass owners bought

"At last, on July 6, 1899, the last spike was driven in the White Pass & Yukon Route's railroad at Lake Bennett. Two paddlewheelers joined the party, one of which was the Australian." (*This caption was supplied by the photographer on the scene, E. A. Hegg, but apparently, from records of the railroad company, this photo was of steel finally reaching Lake Bennett. The "golden spike" was driven a year later, July 29, 1900, at Carcross, and at that time the first train was dispatched over the route.*)

E. A. HEGG

out the remaining companies for $150,000. In January a crew was sent up the pass to tear down the tramways. The crew began at Crater Lake and used the lines from there to Canyon City to haul the gear out. It was April before they completed the task, leaving only the towers and power-station buildings as a reminder of the $175,000 system.

In that same April a botanist named J. A. Tarleton crossed the Chilkoot and met only two other men during the hike. A year earlier there were several thousand there at a time, and an estimated 30,000 had crossed the pass to the Yukon headwaters. He passed dozens of abandoned cabins and saw signs of life only at Lake Bennett, which had remained a settlement due to the railroad equipment and section gangs stationed there.

The post office established in 1896 in Dyea closed its doors forever in 1902, and in 1906 only one man lived in the decaying town. E. A. Klatt had staked a homestead that included part of Dyea and had taken up residence in one of the vacant buildings. He "improved" the area by tearing up and burning down most of the town, selling what pieces he could to Skagway citizens. Although his agricultural activities yielded bumper crops of vegetables, there was no convenient market and he had to abandon the sad town.

Dyea, Canyon City, Pleasant Camp, Finnegans Point, Sheep Camp, Stone House, Long Hill, The Scales, the Golden Stairs, Crater Lake, Long Lake, Happy Camp, Deep Lake, Lake Lindeman—all became memories for crusty old stampeders who alternately enthralled and bored listeners with yarns about that great, mad winter of 1897-98.

The trail soon disappeared in the dense underbrush of Southeast Alaska. The paths worn in the fragile tundra high on the Canadian side of the trail slowly healed. Timber replaced the acres of stumps on the lake shores. The stoves and the books and the strange, primitive motor vehicles were consigned to the elements. Chilkoot Pass wasn't forgotten all those years, but it was ignored.

CHAPTER 17
SKAGWAY AFTERWARDS

When a town is built for a single purpose—whether it be for gold or cattle or fishing—and the reason for its existence disappears, the town is usually doomed. Were it not for the White Pass & Yukon Route, Skagway most certainly would have died as swiftly as Dyea. But a few veterans of the stampede clung to Skagway with the same barnaclelike stubbornness that is a trademark of Alaska and Yukon pioneers.

Some had nothing to return to, and others stayed because they liked Skagway, whether it was a boom town or a community that by today's standards would qualify for federal aid as a disaster area.

One who stayed was Harriet Pullen, who came as a cook for Captain Moore's pier-building crew and ended up owning Moore's home, which she turned into the Pullen House, a rambling and elegant hotel and museum. Mrs. Pullen was probably Skagway's most distinguished and respected citizen throughout those lean years after the rush, and it was rare that a visitor to Skagway did not return home with glowing reports about her hotel, her character and the quality of her rooms and meals.

The population that once was estimated to exceed 15,000 dropped drastically and stabilized at around 500. It surged upward again briefly during World War II when the Alaska Highway was constructed, but it was a temporary boom. Its business was, and still is, tied closely to the Yukon Territory. It serves as the territory's saltwater port through which passes

The railroad ran down the middle of Skagway's main street.

Skagway in about 1910 looks much the same as it does today, except the railroad tracks are gone from the street.

heavy equipment to the mines and towns, and ore from the mines to other parts of the world.

During the 1920s cruise ships began calling at Skagway with stopovers long enough for visitors to tour the town and take day-long rides on the WP&YR chair cars to Lake Bennett for a lunch, and return.

In Skagway the visitors were greeted by one of Alaska's most beloved characters, Martin Itjen, a tour guide, Ford dealer, inventor of Rube Goldberg contraptions, undertaker and Skagway promoter. He also was an intentionally terrible poet.

Itjen stampeded to the Klondike through Skagway in 1897 after news of the strike reached his hometown of Jacksonville, Florida. He failed to strike it rich, and after a variety of jobs, became an undertaker. Complaining that the climate was too healthy to make his business prosper, he got interested in tourism.

Not one to do things halfway, the small man with a distinctive longhorn moustache rigged up a trolley car contraption on a Ford chassis (he invented the body but "Henry" built the chassis), installed a stuffed bear cub with electric eyes and hauled tourists around town with a running commentary about the history of the area and its glorious eccentrics.

Itjen took off once for Hollywood with his trolley and lined up a date with Mae West. His so-bad-it-is-good poetry tells the story well:

> She said to me, "Now Martin,
> If it wasn't for your wife
> I'd take you and your moustache
> For the rest of my sweet life.
>
> "But I'm different from the other movie gals
> For I took a solemn vow
> That I would never come between
> A husband and his frau."

Thus, Martin Itjen escaped the temptations of Hollywood with the help of a lady's virtue. But in the process, Skagway and Itjen received a lot of publicity, which was the reason he went there.

Skagway also received its share of "bad press" during those lean years from tourists and travel writers accustomed to Grand Tour

Skagway.

F. H. NOWELL

accommodations. The townspeople retained a take-us-as-we-are attitude and made no attempts to present Skagway as anything other than what it was—a gold rush town without a gold rush. But generally speaking, it managed to hold its own and found an appreciative group of visitors.

Its rough-and-ready reputation was further reinforced shortly after the gold rush was over when an unusual bit of justice was dealt to a gambler. The nameless gent had lost heavily at the popular gambling hall, appropriately named the Board of Trade, and, as Itjen explained it, "thought he'd come over to the bank and get some more money." Since he had no account at the bank, he took along a gun in one hand and two sticks of dynamite in the other. The cashier refused to honor his withdrawal request, so the gambler fired a shot at him. The dynamite was terribly unstable and it exploded.

The cashier was uninjured, but the bank was a shambles. The gambler was in worse shape because only his head could be found.

The banker was a practical sort so he hosed down the interior of the bank, then dug up the street outside, hauled everything

Dyea had wharves, too, but never as extensive as Skagway's.

down to the Skagway River and built sluice boxes to reclaim the gold dust scattered by the blast. Most of it was recovered.

The gambler was a stranger to everyone in town, so his head was preserved in case a relative or friend should pass through and recognize him. To be certain nobody would miss seeing it, the head was displayed in a museum until 1926, when it was finally buried. The unfortunate mishap occurred in 1900, so the citizens of Skagway can't be accused of haste in burying the evidence. Nor could they be accused of lacking sentiment when an inscription was carved on his headstone:

> *The nob of the man is all that is here.*
> *Will look for the rest when we get over there.*

That inscription is not the only commemoration of the human drama of Skagway's early days. A bronze medallion set in the corner of a building at Sixth and Union in Seattle reads:

> *Mrs. Hannah Newman*
> *With courage and faith in the*
> *development of our city owned*
> *this ground from pioneer days*
> *until the erection of this building.*

And that's all. Therein lies a strange tale of love, jealousy and murder, dating back to the Klondike gold rush.

Molly (or Mollie) Walsh was a pretty Irish colleen who opened a grub tent on the White Pass Trail, and it has been said her face, figure and personality brought in as many customers as her cooking. One of the men who stopped by was "Packer Jack" Newman, who ran a mule train over the pass. He immediately fell in love with her and hung around her tent as much as he could.

But, alas, she had another admirer, a faro dealer in Skagway who wrote Packer Jack a note telling him to stay away from Molly. That didn't set well with Packer Jack. He solved the problem by stopping by to see the faro dealer, and shot him dead. There was no trial. Skagway was that kind of town during the fall and winter of 1897-98.

With one rival out of the way, another appeared, named Mike Bartlett, also a packer on the White Pass Trail. Believing he had some rights to Molly—after all, he had just killed a man over her—Jack ordered her to keep Bartlett away from her tent. But she was a stubborn lass and told Packer Jack she would let anyone in her tent she wanted to serve—for grub only, presumably, since she was a virtuous girl, we are told. Molly wanted to get married one day, but wasn't certain Packer Jack was the man for her since he drank and had even killed a man. So she married Mike Bartlett and moved into Skagway. When the White Pass & Yukon Route was built, the railroad put Packer Jack and Mike out of business. Both men had earned in excess of $100,000 with their pack trains though, an incredible fortune in those days. Molly and Mike moved to Seattle, while Jack settled down in Skagway.

But Molly's marriage went sour and she took off to Mexico with a man named John F. Lynch. They took most of Mike's money with them. When it ran out, she returned to Seattle and, with her husband again, lived with a family named Klien in an alley between Seventh and Eighth near Pike Street.

Below left—To keep the peace with his wife, Hannah, who was understandably nettled by the monument to Molly Walsh, Packer Jack commissioned this plaque in Skagway. It evidently repaired her wounded ego. Below right—Monument erected in Skagway by Packer Jack Newman to the memory of his lost love of the gold rush days, Mollie Walsh.

ALASKA DEPARTMENT OF ECONOMIC DEVELOPMENT
AND PLANNING

On the night of October 27, 1902, Claude G. Bannick, the first mounted policeman in Seattle, saw a woman run through a gate screaming. Before the policeman could get his horse in motion, a man appeared, raised a pistol and fired at the fleeing woman. When he saw her fall, the man turned his weapon on himself. The woman was Molly; her assailant, Mike. Molly died before she reached the hospital. Mike survived the tragedy and blamed someone named Shorty, but would say no more. Mike was sent to an insane asylum, diagnosed as suffering from "dementia." He was released 2 years later, and committed suicide soon after.

Packer Jack Newman remained in love with Molly through the years despite being married to a woman named Hannah. He commissioned an attractive bust of his lost love that stands in Skagway's Molly Walsh Park on 6th Street. The inscription reads:

> *Alone without help this courageous girl ran a grub tent near Log Cabin during the gold rush of 1897-1898. She fed and lodged the wildest gold-crazed men generations shall surely know. This inspiring spirit murdered Oct. 27, 1902.*

Mrs. Newman had had enough. She demanded a plaque for herself, and knowing when to do as he was told, Packer Jack commissioned the medallion we see today on the corner of Sixth and Union in Seattle. It doesn't really say much, but it does pay his debt to Hannah, which is all she wanted anyway.

Among other things, Skagway has the distinction of being the first town to become incorporated in Alaska—on June 28, 1900. Juneau was one day behind it. But its principal product—history—has suffered over the years. Some of its most historic buildings have become dilapidated beyond the point of restoration. The handsome Pullen House has deteriorated beyond hope of repair, and others were torn down or burned.

However, the bulk of the historical district still stands and its 1897-98 charm remains intact. Boardwalks line the dirt main street and storefronts, in most cases, are little different than they were during the great stampede or after the turn of the century when the town stabilized into a place for people to live rather than exploit and move on.

Martin Itjen's trolley-truck is retired, but his spirit lives on as residents steeped in solid history and frivolous nonsense take visitors on tours of museums, the cemetery where Soapy Smith and Frank Reid are buried, and the "Days of '98" show in the Eagle Hall. Dan McGrew is riddled with bullets each night, stories both true and false are told and nobody goes home broke from the funny-money gambling tables.

Although most of the 20th-century amenities are common in Skagway, it really hasn't changed much from the old days just after the stampede. Its citizens realize that its present, and its future, is solidly based on its past. No matter what else happens to the town, what industries should come in or what coming generations might want, it is extremely unlikely that it will ever lose that gold-rush flavor for which it is so famous.

PART II:
THE CHILKOOT TODAY

CHAPTER 18
THE KLONDIKE GOLD RUSH NATIONAL HISTORICAL PARK

It has been half a century in the making, but a park commemorating the Klondike gold rush and preserving sections of the route from Puget Sound to the goldfields outside Dawson City has at last become a reality. It is the Klondike Gold Rush National Historical Park.

The idea first surfaced in 1933 when a group of Skagway citizens appointed by the Skagway Chamber of Commerce approached the National Park Service about establishing either a park or national monument in Skagway and Dyea, on the Chilkoot Trail and portions of the White Pass Trail. The proposal was pigeonholed by the park service because its director at the time, Arno B. Cammerer, mistakenly thought it would be too similar to the Glacier Bay National Monument.

But the idea was kept alive by the territorial delegation in Washington, D.C., and Skagway citizens. Harold L. Ickes became Secretary of the Interior and favored the project, but the park service remained unenthusiastic and let the issue languish in filing cabinets for another 28 years.

When Alaska was admitted to the Union in 1959, the project was revived and a series of trips to Skagway by park service planners and historians gave momentum to Skagway's hopes. The Canadian Department of Indian Affairs and Northern Development expressed a strong interest in cooperating with the Americans and taking over the park from the summits of Chilkoot and White passes and on down the Yukon to Dawson City.

Finally, in the summer of 1976, President Gerald Ford signed a bill creating the park. In essence, the legislation provides for restoration and preservation of Skagway's historic district, the establishment of a visitor center in Skagway, rangers to patrol the Chilkoot Trail during the summer months and the construction of turnouts with interpretative material on the Carcross-Skagway road which follows the White Pass route.

Another element was added to the park: an interpretative center in Seattle's Pioneer Square. This unit of the Klondike park explains the role Seattle played in the gold rush, and has exhibits showing the goods sold in Seattle and the information given about the Klondike in local newspapers at the time. A well-equipped mannequin amid his belongings displays the "ton of goods" required of each man to enter Canada en route to the gold fields.

The center also has valuable information for visitors planning to go on to the Skagway-Chilkoot Pass unit of the park. Lists of equipment needed for the hike, detailed maps and other information will be available. The Seattle interpretative center is at 117 South Main Street, Seattle, Washington 98104.

The Skagway visitor center is a "must" stop for visitors intending to hike the Chilkoot. Here they will be able to obtain the latest information on trail conditions, where to obtain food and equipment in Skagway, the latest customs requirements and other information that will make the trip free of unexpected hitches. This center also has many exhibits and artifacts from the gold-rush days. The mailing address of the Skagway visitor center is: Klondike Gold Rush National Historical Park, Box 517, Skagway, Alaska 99840.

CHAPTER 19
PLANNING YOUR TRIP

The most common direction followed by hikers over the Chiloot Pass is from Skagway into Canada. This is the more natural route, partly because most hikers come from the south and because it was the original approach taken by the stampeders. Also as a practical consideration, the summit is easier to ascend than descend on the American side. Going down the steep scree can be dangerous, and for this reason alone it is best to avoid hiking from the Canadian side south.

You can get to Skagway three ways: By air from Juneau (but not from Whitehorse except charter), by Alaska ferry, or by Klondike Highway 2 that runs from Skagway to Carcross over White Pass to join the Alaska Highway.

On arrival in Skagway you should first check in at the park visitor center, register for the hike and get the latest trail and customs information. Here you can also make arrangements to store gear temporarily or ship it ahead and seek transportation to the trailhead at Dyea. For the inexperienced or faint of heart, you may want to go with the only licensed guide service on the trail: Alaska Discovery, Juneau, AK 99801. It is, however, a good idea to write to the park superintendent well in advance of your departure from home for as much of this information as possible.

As soon as you reach Skagway, it is a good idea to run through your check list again to be sure you have everything you need, such as stove fuel. It is illegal to carry fuel on planes, and it is much easier to find white gasoline or kerosene in Skagway than butane or propane cartridges. Carry four days' supply of fuel because fires are not permitted in Canada, and only in fire rings in Alaska.

Skagway has good supermarkets for all standard items of food and clothing, but you should buy your freeze-dried or dehydrated trail food before leaving for Alaska. Some items are available in Whitehorse for backpackers. Find out in advance how much food you are permitted to bring into Canada. Customs regulations tend to vary from season to season and inspector to inspector.

If you take your own vehicle to Skagway, there is a parking area for visitors with cars near the ranger station in Dyea.

Downtown Skagway.

Chapter 20
THE TRAIL

Your hike begins at the steel bridge that crosses the Taiya River 8.5 miles from Skagway. If you arrive at the trailhead early in the day, you might want to make a short hike down to the old Dyea townsite, which is about 1.5 miles from the bridge. There isn't much left of the townsite—a few piles of rotting lumber, the string of piling stubs leading out across the flats to saltwater and little else.

Of more interest is the Slide Cemetery, which is reached by following the main road to the first fork, then taking the right turn at each junction until you see a sign. The small cemetery has been cleaned up by Skagway citizens and names repainted on wooden grave markers.

The actual trailhead is on a dike road leading from the bridge to the edge of the forest. And when you enter the willows along the river on the trail, you run head-on into a very steep climb that is accepted by Chilkoot veterans as the initiation to the trail. It seems virtually straight up for nearly .25 mile. Part of the problem, undoubtedly, is that you haven't had a chance to get warmed up to the hike. Also, most inexperienced hikers tend to start off fast and strong and won't slow down even though they're beginning to huff and puff.

After topping the ridge over the river, the trail levels off into a series of up and down sections that aren't particularly taxing. The trail is high above the Taiya River along here and occasionally you are out of hearing range of the water. Huge granite boulders, windfall, spruce and brush are seen along the side of the 5,000-

foot A-B Mountain. Across the Taiya you can occasionally see a road called West Creek Road that dead-ends a short distance upriver.

After hiking about .5 mile, the trail drops back down to the river level and runs over relatively smooth ground for the next 3 miles. At Mile 1.6 the trail connects with an old logging road and the walking is very easy until Mile 3. There, the remains of an old sawmill with two old shacks and big sawdust piles offer a good spot to prepare lunch. A small, sluggish stream is about 100 feet uptrail from the sawmill site, the closest water.

If you start your hike in the afternoon, the sawmill site is adequate for an overnight stop, although the mosquito and noseeum population is usually quite high due to the still water.

Dyea Inlet.

"Dancehall girl" of the Gay '90s show in Skagway.

Beyond the sawmill, the old road continues its relatively level run until you reach, at about Mile 4.9, the place known as Finnegans Point. In this general area, an entrepreneur named Finnegan and his sons constructed a corduroy road over marshy terrain and charged $2 each for people to use it. Reportedly, when the stampede reached hordelike proportions, they simply ignored the Finnegans. This is also the first place you can camp.

Across the Taiya River from Finnegans Point one can see Irene Glacier on the mountain with streams tumbling down the steep slope on their way to the Taiya.

A short distance ahead, the trail again begins a series of rises and descents, first down to the river's edge, then up through gaps in the granite boulders, then down steep sections with handrails and over bridges.

At Mile 7.0 the trail crosses a wide stretch of old riverbed with moss and lichen-covered rocks, and an occasional spruce trying to

Rows of piling stubs at Dyea townsite.

The Slide Cemetery at Dyea.

survive in the barren soil. Wild flowers may be seen early in the summer. The trail has been clearly marked here by small stones lining it like a cottage path. Frequently the trail enters the timber again to run beside bogs lush with fern and devil's club, then back out into riverbed again.

The Canyon City shelter isn't visible until one is almost upon it, and the last few steps across the bridge into the clearing around the cabin are among the sweetest of the hike. A fast stream flows past the shelter, and less than a hundred yards up the stream is a series of beautiful waterfalls.

The shelter is made of logs with a corrugated roof that

The historic cemetery in Skagway is best known for the graves of Soapy Smith and Frank Reid. Reid's headstone is the tall one at the right of the young man in the photo.

Above Canyon City, the Taiya River sometimes is compressed into a gorge so narrow you can almost step across it.

overhangs the front to form a porch. It is equipped with eight bunks, a table, benches, wood stove and cupboard space. Because it is so gloomy inside the cabin, most hikers prefer to set up tents outside and store their packs on the porch. Cooking is virtually impossible on the stove so don't depend on it.

Outside is a pit toilet that smells no better or worse than other pit toilets. The pack-it-in, pack-it-out ethic should be strictly observed here as at all campsites along the trail.

Many hikers make Canyon City their first campsite on the trail, and as a result, it is getting to be rather crowded at the peak of summer. There are other campsites suitable for overnight use just beyond the shelter that offer more privacy.

Just over .5 mile uptrail from the shelter is a suspension bridge that leads across the Taiya to the original Canyon City site. A much-used campsite is at the trail side of the bridge. The Canyon City townsite is the first collection of ruins you encounter that date back to the gold rush. A selection of cooking utensils, an old stove or two, a few collapsed cabins and garbage dumps are around the area. The town was built on moraine or old stream-bed and hasn't been taken over by the timber and underbrush as Sheep Camp has been.

A hiker approaching the Canyon City shelter.

An abandoned cookstove at Canyon City.

But the centerpiece of the town is the old steam boiler left behind by the WP&YR crews that wrecked the towns from the summit of Dyea when the railroad bought the tramways and demolished them.

The boiler apparently was used for an electric power plant, since some accounts of the gold rush mention electric lights in Canyon City and Sheep Camp.

Sections of the smokestack lie nearby, and there is evidence the boiler was moved a short distance from its moorings. Whether the WP&YR crews moved it a few feet, then abandoned the effort, or someone in later years tried to haul it out and gave up probably will never be known.

From the suspension bridge, the main trail runs along fairly moderately, then heads upward again through the boulders and back down again to cross streams on footbridges. Occasionally you will see stretches of telegraph wire lying beside the trail or swaying down from trees.

You will encounter another steep climb about a mile beyond the Canyon City bridge. At the top of the climb, you can look backward for a final glimpse of saltwater at Lynn Canal, visible on clear days.

During the early summer you are likely to see hummingbirds along this portion of the trail, to which they migrate each year. It is thought that Lake Lindeman is the farthest north nesting ground of the rufous hummingbird.

After topping the steep climb, the trail begins a series of mild up and down stretches, then swings back to the river's edge at an open glen generally known as Camp Pleasant (the original site was across the river). It *is* a pleasant place to camp away from the hordes at Canyon City and Sheep Camp. Apparently several tents

Inspecting the old boiler of a tramway power plant at Canyon City.

were pitched here at various times during the stampede, and it is one of the only open spots on this part of the trail. Again, views of glaciers and waterfalls are offered through the open timber.

The remaining 3 miles to Sheep Camp are relatively easy and little different from the trail you have already covered.

The shelter at Sheep Camp is virtually identical to that at Canyon City. The major difference is the artifacts collected both inside and out. It should be noted here that the park service does not want your help in collecting more! The whole trail is protected under the Antiquities Act.

The crumbling remains of a cabin are near the shelter. A toilet was built beside the cabin, and the Taiya runs less than 100 feet below the door. Tent space is more limited here than at Canyon City because the timber is thicker. The rangers also have a station near here.

The Sheep Camp buildings are, for the most part, across the river from the shelter. The river is divided into several channels at this point. The last channel runs over and between a series of boulders that have been polished smooth by the river.

You can expect to see wild flowers, squirrels, porcupine, an occasional eagle and, infrequently, black and brown bears. Bears have caused no problems on the Chilkoot to date, and local people who know bears' habits doubt that they will, unless the hikers turn the shelter areas into open garbage pits or try to hide their garbage in the brush. The scent of man is firmly embedded into Chilkoot now, and most hikers make enough noise to warn bears of their approach.

Shortly after leaving the Sheep Camp shelter, the trail begins climbing and doesn't really let up until the summit. At about Mile 14.5, or 1.5 miles from Sheep Camp, you leave the timber behind. The trail swings back to the Taiya, by now a small but extremely fast stream that tumbles over rocks. At times the trail leads you across the various channels of the stream, which can become a torrent in a storm.

To the right, or east, is a sheer cliff over which waterfalls of all sizes plunge. And this mountain is the birthplace for the vast talus field over which you must scramble for about 2 miles.

Spotted along the route are big sprockets from the tramways, steel telegraph poles embedded in the rocks but bent crazily by avalanches. Here you must rely on the small cairns and wands

A sprocket from the tramway, near Sheep Camp.

placed daily by rangers to mark the best trail, and in their absence, follow the path of least resistance over the boulders, keeping close to the stream.

At Mile 15.5 are the first ruins of any significance above timber line. Perched across the stream on a ledge are a collapsed building and a tramway tripod. It is believed the building was a tramway office, restaurant and store. Directly across the Taiya River is the first level spot since leaving timber line, and a convenient place to stop for lunch. This area often has snowstorms during June and July.

One should use extreme caution crossing snow bridges over the stream, and parties should spread out at least 50 feet apart while on the snow. It is particularly dangerous near the edge and where rocks protrude. After the snow melts you will have to cross the stream. Here again the rangers will have marked the best route over boulders. Watch your step.

While it is safer to remain in the valley between the cliffs lining the stream, some hikers choose to climb up on the ledge on the west, or left, side of the stream. But one should never leave sight of the trail in case of accident.

The trail follows the spine of a series of ridges up and down until, at last, it drops down into a crescent-shaped bowl beneath the mountains. If the snow has melted, one will see evidence of

Hikers climbing Long Hill.

It isn't known if this is a genuine headstone or something that appeared later. It was found between some boulders above Sheep Camp.

cabins, machinery, cooking utensils, tools, sleds, clothing and other debris rotting slowly away. This is The Scales.

One approaches The Scales at a slight angle, and it is easy to become confused if the weather is bad, which is more often the

Crossing a snowfield beneath the remains of a tramway powerhouse and tripod-shaped cable support.

From The Scales, the Chilkoot climb is the first pronounced notch at the left. One goes straight ahead from where the photographer was standing, then angles slightly to the left up the boulder pile. The other notch, the Petterson Trail, is potentially dangerous and not recommended. It is unmarked and the rocks are unstable.

case than not. As you stand at The Scales, the summit will be slightly to your left rather than straight ahead as one would suspect.

As you leave The Scales and start for the summit, to the right will be the Petterson Trail, which curves around to the left and back up toward the summit. This route is not recommended because rocks are very unstable and the trail is not marked. The Chilkoot, or the Golden Stairs, is the cut in the mountain before the Petterson.

If you are in doubt, wait until you can see the top before proceeding. The Chilkoot has loose boulders all the way to the top, and cable left over from the tramways is lying on the rocks. On the cliffs above the trail are some old tramway supports still protruding from the rocks.

Follow the markers up the Golden Stairs, picking your way

Scrambling over the boulders of the summit climb in a whiteout. Old cables from the tramway at right can be used as guides in foul weather, along with orange or yellow triangles on aluminum rods placed as markers by the rangers.

among the boulders carefully. Whichever route you take, at least part of the way will be an all-fours situation because it is so steep.

After you've climbed about three-fourths of the way up, you will come to a level spot behind some boulders. It is a good place to regroup and to stop for photographs if the weather permits. Lying on the boulders just above the dropping-off point are the remains of a motorized sled, or some such contraption. Some believe it belonged to Archie Burns, the first of the tramway operators.

After regrouping, the rest of the summit climb is up a rather mild grade, through a narrow gap near the monument (Mile 16.5) dedicated in 1965 by Gov. Walter Hickel to the stampeders. The monument was built by Boy Scouts, and is only a few yards from the actual summit marker, a plate that is usually under the snow. On a ledge to the right (east), above the monument, is a cache of wood-and-canvas collapsible canoes that had been a mystery to Chilkoot hikers and historians from the gold rush to the present.

The mystery was partially solved when Dr. Robert E. King, an

These collapsible canoes at the summit have long been a matter of conjecture, but recent research by an archaeologist revealed the owner and information on the "nonpariel canvas compartment boats."

WENDY WOLF

archaeologist working for the National Park Service, discovered a bill of sale for the boats that had been filed in the Skagway City Hall on June 10, 1898.

The Flowers, Smith & Company had sold several articles, such as marine engines, parts of a steam launch *and* "232 nonpariel canvas compartment boats, together with oars, rowlocks and other material for the aforesaid boats; also 49 Chicago Sectional Metal boats together with all lockers, canvas, oars and material used in the construction and equipment of the aforesaid boats."

It is possible that one of the Chicago Sectional Metal boats was left behind near Deep Lake. At least two of the wood-and-canvas boats have been removed from the summit cache. One boat was placed in the Soapy Smith Museum in Skagway and the other was reassembled in the visitors center in Skagway.

Actually, collapsible canoes were fairly common during that period and some contemporary accounts mention them so casually that one assumes that canoes were taken for granted along the route north.

If you are in luck, when you start down from the summit the Canadian Chilkoot will be laid out in bright sunlight in all its alpine glory. But don't be surprised if a cloud cover extends on toward Bennett. Crater Lake is first, often iced in until August, and incredibly blue when the ice is gone. The snow usually persists until near the lake, and you catch yourself hurrying down the slopes to the lake faster than you should. And if you haven't trimmed your toenails before striking out on the trip, here is where you wish you had. This is a steep descent on either snow or rocks.

The first stop for most hikers usually is the crumbling rock crib just above the lake. It formerly anchored a tramway, and was the northern terminus for freight going north. A cabin adjoined it, now a pile of rotten boards and logs, and just beneath the crib is a crushed metal boat. This is a good place to stop for a rest and a cup of tea or coffee. Several small three-person shelters are in the area.

Frequently the summit area will be socked in, but at Crater Lake, .5 mile away, the sun is likely to be shining as the clouds whip through the pass and over the mountaintops, only to dissipate in the dry air of Canada. But not always, so don't plan on it.

Crater Lake on a calm, clear day.

Crater Lake is ringed with ruins from the stampede, some easy to spot, others obscured by the years. After leaving the crib, one of the first signs is a series of tent sites in a marshy area. They are marked by poles laid down as tent bases. Off to the west, or left, at water's edge is a larger metal boat, also crushed by snow.

At Mile 19, almost 3 miles from the summit, are the remains of a teamster's headquarters beside the lake. If the snow is still covering the ground, it will be easy to miss. When the snow is gone, a few wagon wheels and scraps of lumber are seen lying on the ground. These should not be touched. Just above them on a narrow shelf is a patch of prairie grass growing where the teamster had a barn or shed. It is the only such patch of grass in the area and it is assumed it grew from the supply of hay the teamster kept there for his horses.

From the teamster's headquarters looking toward Long Lake you will see wagon tracks where he hauled goods from the ferry on Crater Lake to the ferry on Long Lake.

At the same place is an island with a stone causeway built out to it which some believe was the ferry dock.

The trail from Crater Lake past a small lake (some call it Blue Lake, others, Morrow Lake) and on down to the canyon just before Long Lake is easy hiking, and beautiful hiking as well. The plant life here is limited mainly to varieties of heather, moss and lichen, but with profuse wild flowers thrown in for decoration in late summer. The heather frequently blooms just after the snow melts, and a close-up attachment for your camera will be appreciated here.

Just before you enter the canyon near Long Lake, Coltsfoot Creek tumbles down a picturesque waterfall, often from beneath a snowbank. Here, 5 miles from the summit, is Happy Camp, aptly named after the trek from Sheep Camp. An outhouse has been built here to encourage camping (and cats' manners). The stream flattens out in the canyon and has an easy trip into Long Lake. Hikers do not. They must scramble over loose rock beside the stream for about .25 mile before the trail comes to an opening where some small trees grow in a ravine.

Many hikers believe the next mile and a half is the most beautiful portion of the whole journey. The trail zigzags upward about 350 feet to the shelf over Long Lake and dips and swerves between tarns, hat-sized ponds, through stunted alpine fir and hemlock that looks as though a Japanese master gardener laid it out. Each tarn is so clear one sometimes has the feeling one is

An abandoned and crushed boat on Crater Lake. Apparently the heavy snow crushed it, but why it was left behind is a mystery.

Early in the hiking season, Crater Lake is surrounded by deep snowbanks.

The trail is littered with shoes and boots that were worn out and discarded.

A teamster had a barn at this site. Seeds from his store of hay apparently dropped beneath the floor, began growing and are still regenerating themselves.

Wagon tracks still show at Blue Lake, between Crater and Long lakes, where the teamster hauled freight in 1897-98.

The remains of two wagons at a teamster's headquarters beside Crater Lake.

looking through a pane of glass rather than water, and some have one or two small stones on the bottom as though they were placed by an aquatic interior designer.

At the end of Long Lake, the trail begins another series of switchbacks down to water level again, and Deep Lake is stretched out below. The first footbridge on the Canadian side crosses the stream connecting Long and Deep lakes. Directly above the bridge is an excellent campsite sheltered by the trees and with an outhouse. There are other campsites on top of the cliff overlooking the lake.

Deep Lake is an island-studded, double lake with a marshy shore and occasional sandy points protruding into it. The trail follows the shore through low fir trees and opens up on the cliff above the lake's outlet, Moose Creek. Here, Mile 23.5, is the metal frame of a knockdown canoe held together by bolts, and pieces of wooden and metal sleds.

Directly below these implements is a high waterfall, where Moose Creek literally falls out of the lake. The trail skirts the rim above the canyon, occasionally dropping back into the timber, then swinging out to the very edge of the cliff. Numerous waterfalls can be seen, and it is worth the effort to leave the trail and walk down to the edge for photographs of the falls and rapids. Exercise caution, however.

At Mile 25 the trail passes the ruins of two or three cabins. Near the cabins are some stumps about 6 feet tall. These trees were cut by stampeders during the winter of 1897-98 when the snow was deep, and dropped over the cliff into the river to be floated down to Lake Lindeman for boatbuilding. Several other stumps 5 or 6 feet high can be found in the Lindeman City area, relics of that same winter. Beyond the cabins the trail passes a small lake and crosses the narrow outlet.

The trail swings back into the timber and doesn't emerge again until Lake Lindeman and the Lindeman City townsite are directly below. As you begin the descent you can see the lake spread out beneath the mountain range on the far shore. Below, at the edge

Many of the pieces of equipment discarded or broken during the gold rush show remarkable workmanship, such as this section of a sled.

Coltsfoot Creek connects Crater and Long lakes and flows through steep-walled Coltsfoot Canyon. This section of trail, over snow ledges at breakup in June and later on loose rock, can be dangerous.

Sleds and the shell of a boat were left at Deep Lake. The boat was constructed of steel ribs bolted together and covered with canvas.

Below Deep Lake the stream drops down a series of rapids into a narrower canyon below the trail.

The trail swings around a point and gives a panoramic view of Lake Lindeman and the mountains surrounding it.

of the lake, is one of the two cabins built by the Yukon government for hikers.

Lake Lindeman is a good place for a layover if you have extra time. You can catch up on your washing of both clothing and sweaty bodies, and take leg-limbering day hikes back into the timber and along the lake's shore. Here you have some of the best camping on the trail in the open timber, and the cabin can be used for drying clothes in bad weather or as a communal house. The cabin is almost exactly on the site where the Royal North-West Mounted Police barracks stood.

Scattered around the area are remains of several other buildings. Numerous artifacts are lying around, and should be left lying around.

Off the main trail, a winding trail passes beneath the Lake Lindeman Cemetery and leads to the cabin built by the Yukon government at the mouth of Moose Creek on the lake.

One side hike from Lindeman, unmarked on maps, is along the lake shore back toward Chilkoot and up the opposite side of the ridge of the trail. Remains of old cabins and another boiler (where did they all come from?) are lying around the rocks up there. The trail originally followed the ridge rather than the rim of the canyon.

Another cabin built by the Yukon government for modern hikers is about .5 mile down the lake from the first, at the mouth of the stream that comes down from Deep Lake. It is more remote than the Lindeman City cabin, and for those few who pack fishing equipment over the pass, offers so-so fishing. Since fishing is usually poor, it is probably not worth it. Also, you need British Columbia fishing licenses.

The trail from Lake Lindeman cuts almost due east to a high bridge across the stream, then up a ridge to relatively barren and rocky sections with more views of the lake. At Mile 27.5 is another, smaller lake with peninsulas protruding into it that make

The Presbyterian Church on the hill overlooking Lake Bennett.

A view of the north end of Lake Lindeman with Prospectors Mountain to the left.

good campsites. But the lake is getting heavy use; be warned you might not be alone. Also, it hosts a healthy bug population.

From this lake (some call it Bare Loon Lake), the trail is mostly over rocky ground and one has to be careful because the footing can be tricky. It is 7 miles from Lindeman to Bennett. Here a trail leads to the railroad tracks and out to Log Cabin.

Other than the shell of the church, there isn't much from the gold rush era remaining at Bennett. Some cabin sites dug out of the sandy bank above the lake are about the only other remains.

The White Pass & Yukon Route ceased operation after the 1982 season, and at this writing appears to be out of business entirely. This means that Chilkoot hikers must make their own arrangements for transportation via the highway before they leave Skagway.

To reach the Klondike Highway 2 from trail's end at Bennett, you will have to walk seven miles back up the WP&YR roadbed

to where it intersects with the highway.

Various plans for hikers' transportation are being discussed, including a plan to run the trains during the summer months for the tourist industry. But it is most likely that shuttle buses will operate on a scheduled basis from Skagway to where the railroad and highway intersect.

Check with the National Park Service, either in Skagway or the Seattle Klondike Park unit, before leaving.

A group that hiked the Chilkoot is shown heading down Lake Bennett in a powered inflatable boat, en route to Dawson City. More and more people are following the entire "Trail of '98" from Skagway to Dawson City each summer. The 600-plus-mile trip takes you down Lake Bennett and through Tagish and Marsh lakes, and then down the Yukon River through Whitehorse, the length of Lake Laberge, and past numerous ghost towns that were populated until the Klondike Highway was built in the 1950s, which put the river steamboats out of business.

Chilkoot Good Manners

Since man appears to be the only species that cannot live in the wilderness without endangering it, and since he has a great deal in common with pack rats, a few precautionary notes should be sounded here.

Garbage left on the trail will never become artifacts; today's junk will remain junk and it will not enhance the area's historical interest. If you take something in with you, be sure it goes out again.

The high country is especially fragile and the lakes above Lindeman are virtually sterile. So do not wash dishes in them, and when digging trench latrines, be certain they will not drain into the lake. Dig another trench to dump dishwater into.

Don't wander off the trail in the high country. A footprint can easily become a bog, then a stream. The plant life has a difficult time surviving, and heavy boots won't help.

Leave all artifacts for someone else to see, and remember the Antiquities Act and its fines.

Don't move the trail markers. The words aren't especially beautiful or natural. But they are the only thing you can see in the foul weather that is frequent in the summit area.

Always clean cabins before leaving.

Always leave a good supply of firewood and kindling at the cabins.

Whenever possible, leave a few matches behind, but put them in a mouse- or porcupine-proof container, or hang them from the ceiling in a plastic bag.

If there are no candles in the cabin, leave one if you can spare it. Most hikers carry them, but we can be our brother's keeper if it doesn't risk our own safety.

Treat the Chilkoot Trail as if it were an outdoor museum, because it actually is.

Chilkoot Equipment

Hikers have their own check list of equipment if they are experienced backpackers; if they aren't, they shouldn't be on the Chilkoot without someone with that experience. However, there are a few basic items one should carry.

Compass, sheath knife, suit of lightweight rain clothing (nylon, not plastic; coats and pants, not ponchos), spare socks, a small stove with ample fuel for 4 days or more, small first-aid kit, lightweight tent with rain fly, wool shirt and pants, warm sleeping bag, food for 4 days and emergency rations (don't nibble into them!), gloves or mittens, suntan lotion and sunglasses.

You might also consider carrying a set of crampons, and an ice ax is convenient both for cutting steps in steep snowbanks and as a staff. You should wear boots with lug soles. In most circumstances, lug soles will get you across the snow.

Do not plan on finding shelter in the cabins. Somebody is probably already there.

Do not plan on finding wood stoves for your cooking. You'll eat dry or cold food. Pretend cabins and wood stoves do not exist. You must be completely self-sufficient.

Air rescues are at your own expense. They are terribly expensive (one recent helicopter rescue cost exactly $750.12).

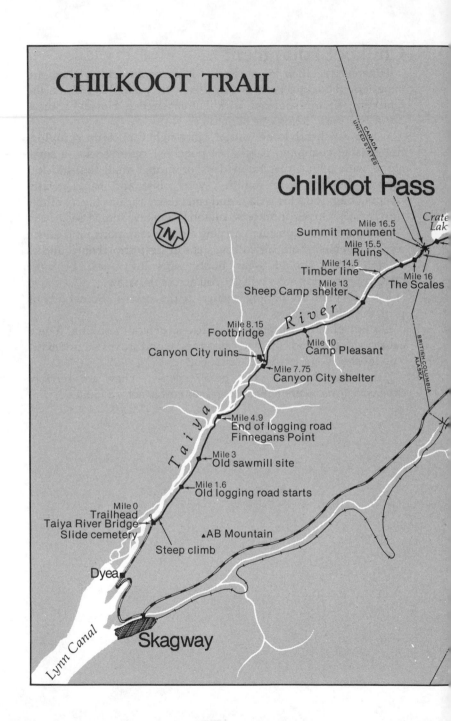

CHILKOOT TRAIL

Chilkoot Pass

Crate Lak

Mile 16.5
Summit monument

Mile 15.5
Ruins

Mile 14.5
Timber line

Mile 13
Sheep Camp shelter

Mile 16
The Scales

Mile 8.15
Footbridge

Canyon City ruins

Mile 10
Camp Pleasant

Mile 7.75
Canyon City shelter

Mile 4.9
End of logging road
Finnegans Point

Mile 3
Old sawmill site

Mile 1.6
Old logging road starts

Mile 0
Trailhead
Taiya River Bridge
Slide cemetery

Steep climb

▲AB Mountain

Dyea

Skagway

Lynn Canal

Taiya River

Taiya

CANADA
UNITED STATES

BRITISH COLUMBIA
ALASKA

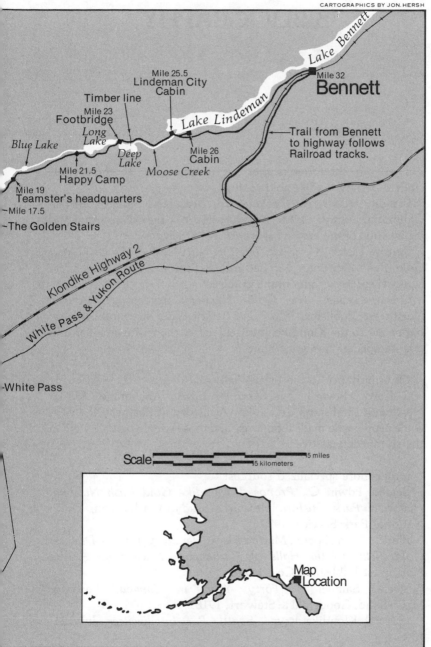

Lake Bennett

Mile 25.5
Lindeman City
Cabin

■ Mile 32
Bennett

Timber line

Lake Lindeman

Mile 23
Footbridge

*Long
Lake*

Blue Lake

*Deep
Lake*

Trail from Bennett
to highway follows
Railroad tracks.

Mile 26
Cabin

Moose Creek

Mile 21.5
Happy Camp

Mile 19
Teamster's headquarters

Mile 17.5

The Golden Stairs

Klondike Highway 2

White Pass & Yukon Route

White Pass

Scale

5 miles

5 kilometers

Map
Location

209

BIBLIOGRAPHY

There are three books that are indispensable to the serious student of the Klondike gold rush:

Wright, Allen A. *Prelude to Bonanza.* Sidney, British Columbia: Gray, 1976. A history of the discovery and exploration of the Yukon before the gold rush.

Berton, Pierre. *Klondike: The Life and Death of the Last Great Gold Rush.* Toronto: McClelland & Stewart, 1963. The most comprehensive account of the gold rush.

Green, Lewis. *The Gold Hustlers.* Anchorage: Alaska Northwest Publishing Co., 1977. The only account of what happened to the Klondike goldfields after the rush was over and the stampeders had gone home.

Of importance to the local history:

Clifford, Howard, *The Skagway Story.* Anchorage: Alaska Northwest Publishing Co., 1975. A history of Skagway the city, some people who made it famous, and those who kept it alive when the stampede was over.

Other more specialized sources:

Bearss, Edwin C., *Proposed Klondike Gold Rush National Historical Park; Historic Resource Study.* Washington, D.C.: National Park Service, 1970.

Black, Martha Louise. *Martha Black: Her Story from the Dawson Gold Fields to the Halls of Parliament.* Anchorage: Alaska Northwest Publishing Co., 1976.

Steele, Samuel B. *Forty Years in Canada.* Toronto: McClelland, Goodchild & Stewart, 1918.

"Special Klondike Issue." *Seattle Post-Intelligencer,* July 21, 1898.

INDEX